Chance to Dance

Chance to Dance

Risking a Spiritually Mature Life

by W. Robert McClelland

CBP Press
St. Louis, Missouri

© Copyright 1986 CBP Press

Second printing, 1989

All rights reserved. No part of this book may be reproduced by any method without the publisher's written permission. Address:

CBP Press
Box 179
St. Louis, MO 63166

Library of Congress Cataloging in Publication Data

McClelland, W. Robert (William Robert), 1931-
   Chance to dance.

   1. Middle age—Religious life. 2. Middle age. 3. McClelland, W. Robert (William Robert), 1931-
I. Title.
BV4579.5.M35   1986   248.8'4   85-18987
ISBN 0-8272-0449-3

Manufactured in the United States of America

Dedication

To Dottie,
Who through the years
Has remained a classy lady.

Contents

Preface

It is with considerable hesitation that I share these thoughts with you because nothing is more open to misinterpretation than Christian freedom. I lay myself open to misunderstanding by those who have not yet entered the turbulence of mid-life and its accompanying faith crisis. It may be that what is contained in these chapters will be called an invitation to license and a heretical misinterpretation of the scripture. Rather than a statement of faith it may be seen as a confession of apostasy. But I do not offer it as a tome of theology. Rather, it is a diary of experience linking my story with that of our biblical ancestors. I identify with Tolstoy's comment that:

> If I were told I might write a book in which I should demonstrate beyond any doubt the correctness of my opinions on every social problem I should not waste two hours at it; but if I were told that what I wrote would be read twenty years from now by people who are children today and that they would read and laugh over my book and love life more because of it, then I should devote all of my life and strength to such a work.[1]

I trust this little volume will be a joyous statement about life in general and mid-life in particular, one that will enable its readers to love life more for having read it.

In a society that has become increasingly aware of the aging process, we still speak of the mid-life period as a "crisis," a "second childhood," or "middle-aged crazies." I believe the Bible invites us to see this time as "opportunity," "birthing," or "resurrection." It thereby qualitatively redefines our understanding of middle age and beyond. My intention is that *Chance to*

Dance go beyond the many excellent sociological-psychological studies of middle age by offering a uniquely "grace-full" understanding of this time of life, drawing specifically on the wisdom of the Bible. Since the Bible does not present a doctrine of middle age, the treatment of the subject in this book will be insightful rather than systematic.

If there is a central theme to be discerned throughout the treatment, it is that institutionalized religion is a good and necessary scaffold in the early building of a spiritual life. But a time comes (mid-life) when the scaffold needs to be dismantled for the sake of the spiritual life it was intended to serve. This dismantling process calls forth the resistance of religious authority and requires of us courage to risk the consequent anxiety and uncertainty of birthing a spiritually mature life. The biblical perspectives that are opened here, I believe, offer such courage and permission for risking the journey.

While I have written with the middle-aged reader in mind—particularly the Christian middle-aged reader—the book has, I trust, a broader interest for both a younger audience and for those at the fringes of the church and beyond. Anyone involved in the traumatic throes of growth will be able to identify with, and learn from, other pilgrims in a similar situation regardless of age.

The first chapter identifies the traumas of mid-life as God's invitation to dance a new step. But to see the exciting possibilities calls for a new understanding of our dance partner: the purpose of Chapter Two. Chapter Three shows that to dance freely requires God's permission to be a sinner. Therefore, to realize our full spiritual potential, we must break free from social pressures and religious authority in order to keep step with the God of Grace. This is the concern of the last chapter. The work then concludes with a call to risk living the miracle we call life.

But how shall we speak of this God of Grace? The problem of sexist God language is always difficult to resolve. To speak of God abstractly is to lose the personal sense of intimacy, which is important to retain if we are to think of life as a dance and God as our partner. Yet to retain the masculine gender is to exclude not only the feminine side of God but also to confuse the analogy of dancing with God for male readers. To use the "his/hers" or "s/he" is to resort to an awkwardness of language and lose the flow of the sentence. Therefore, I have chosen to use the masculine reference to God in the Introduction and the feminine in Chapter One, alternating genders in each of the succeeding chapters. I trust this will keep God's dual nature before us without artificiality or awkwardness of language.

As in any endeavor, many hands make light work. But especially is this true in the writing of a book. To Jacquie Keeter for her dedication to the arduous task of deciphering my hieroglyphics and typing them into manuscript form, I am deeply indebted. To Bonnie Montle for typing and proofreading the final copy and the many hours spent in chasing down quotations, I owe endless gratitude. To Roland Tapp, Verona Thompson, William Gay, and Kay Seba for their encouragement, comments, and help along the way. And, of course, to Herb Lambert for his helpful suggestions and general oversight of production. Thank you. Beyond specific individuals, are the congregations of Hope, Kirkwood, and Northminster Presbyterian churches in St. Louis, who served as sounding boards for many of the ideas presented here. Without their articulate response, the sharpening of thoughts would have suffered. Finally to you, dear reader, for the honor you do me by cussing and discussing what I have taken the time to share, I am grateful!

W. Robert McClelland
St. Louis, Missouri, 1985

Introduction

Reluctantly I opened my eyes. The reprieve of sleep had been sweet. But the light of a new day nudged me into consciousness. I fought reentry into the restless waves in which I had been swimming, but awareness was already upon me with enough focus to know that I wanted to run. I wanted to jump on a motorcycle and head west—by myself—away from my family, my work, away from responsibilities. I wanted to run away from myself. No longer did I recognize the man in the bathroom mirror. He was a stranger to me.

"Burn out" is a term sometimes used to characterize the feelings that wash the shores of the middle-aged psyche. I was burned out. I had given nearly twenty-five years to the profession of being a clergyperson, ministering to people's spiritual and emotional needs. I had been on call, attentive and available. But as I became more and more preoccupied with my own loss of enthusiasm for work and this vague sense of wanting to run for dear life, people coming to me with their hurts became more and more of a burden.

Not only was I perplexed by the needs of others; I was bewildered by my own. My marriage of over twenty-five years had been a joy and entirely fulfilling. Parenting, perhaps, brought out the worst in me, but my marriage to Dottie had been a "piece of cake." Yet, I found myself being attracted to other women. Not only was I physically attracted to them, but I was emotionally vulnerable to their interest in, and attention to, me. It became increasingly apparent to me why some, trying to navigate the confusing currents of the mid-life seas, find themselves emotionally involved before they realize it and caught in the rip tides of an affair. No doubt the awareness made me a better pastoral counselor, but it was nonetheless unnerving to experience the allure of entering one myself.

As a preaching theologian, I was a student of the great minds of the church: Barth, Bultmann, Niebuhr, Tillich, Bonhoeffer. I was conversant with Calvin and Luther. I had read most of the good commentaries, subscribed to the leading professional journals, and maintained a disciplined study program. It had not been with me as it was with the graduating seminarian who asked Reinhold Niebuhr what to preach about in his first parish. Niebuhr replied, "This Sunday you tell them everything you've learned. It's the next Sunday you have to worry about." I had managed to provide on those "next Sundays"—twenty-five years of them—if not the wisdom of the ages, at least sufficient nourishment to feed the flock. But now I was wrung out. I had nothing more to say. No longer did I hit the pulpit on a dead run, eager to share some new insight into scripture. I had given it my best shots. I was tired. It was not that I awoke one morning aware that I was tired. It was simply that I became increasingly aware of being restless. The challenges of the church had turned to frustrations.

But as disturbing as my own inner confusion was, the discovery that my theological studies had not prepared me for this experience was even more upsetting. They seemed to label my unrest as a loss of faith, wrestling with the Tempter, or a second childhood. Several mentors emerged who were reassuring. Among them were Howard Thurman, Sam Keen, and Paul Tillich. I was aided in my pilgrimage not only by what they said in their theological writings but also by the autobiographical insights that they and others shared, insights which provided the life setting for their theological reflections.

More and more I am convinced that theology at its best is always autobiographical. That is, the theology that is most helpful is not a rational system of thought that stands on its own merits, separate from its creator like an object of art that can be admired or discussed as a thing apart. Rather, theology is an instinctive human enterprise in which we try to make sense of, and understand, our experience in relation to some reference point such as God. That which we experience, and that which we think or say about the experience, are inextricably bound together. Such theology cannot be understood, much less discussed, by someone who has not shared a similar experience. Ambiguities and contradictions may abound in such theology because that is the way life is often experienced.

Good theology is good mental health because it deals with reality—not as it "should" be—but as it really is. A systematic theology, on the other hand, can often be an elaborate construct that proceeds from a basic premise or governing idea, such as the sovereignty of God. Once this idea is granted, all else proceeds logically, connectedly, until a whole system of thought is constructed. The work can be appreciated, the logic argued. But if the basic premise is denied—or more to the point, if the basic premise does not correspond to our experience—we may be able to admire the system but unable to identify with it. There is even the danger that, though we cannot identify with it, we may yet be tyrannized by it. Ideas in print, especially ideas about God, tend to take on an importance that can become authoritative for us. Such authority is external to us. Yet when systems of thought acquire external authority, they can judge our experience, label it, and make us feel guilty about it whenever our experience does not fit into the system.

Take for example the label "sin." When an external authority such as a clergyperson, the church's teaching, or a book labels something "sin," and we grant such labeling the status of authoritative Truth, it can take an event in our experience that is essentially joyful and good and turn it sour by making us feel guilty, not only about the incident itself but also for being so perverse as to have enjoyed it. The incident is labeled "sin" and we are labeled "sinful."

Many tragic stories can be told of good, natural, instinctive behavior that has been disparaged in this way. I remember well such an incident from my childhood. My father, a minister, was offering a prayer of gratitude for the food before us as we sat gathered around the evening dinner table. I was in a happy mood, full of enthusiasm for the play from which I had just been called. As my father prayed, I began beating time to his cadence with my knife and fork. He ceased praying and scolded me for being so disrespectful—not merely to him but to God. I was crushed. My joy was wicked. My enthusiasm was blasphemous. I was a sinful, naughty boy.

From my more mature vantage point, I cannot in my wildest imagination think that God was offended by my sense of rhythm. I rather imagine my performance caused him to reminisce about the "good old days" when the Israelites danced before him, singing and clapping their hands, long before people came to believe that prayer and worship should be solemn. In any case, had I been more mature, I would have trusted my own experience and not been tyrannized by a regrettable, and quite arbitrary, label that grew out of an abstract, but no doubt quite rational, system of thought—and, I might add, a system sincerely held by my father.

Good theology is good mental health, but bad theology—that is, theology that does not grow out of experience—is bad mental health. It creates, and tends to force us into, a fantasy world of ideas and labels, definitions and laws, that are constructed apart from the shared realities of the human adventure.

An external authority, even if it be labeled "God"—perhaps especially if it is labeled "God"—is a tyrant and not to be trusted. The only authority which can be trusted is the God within, whom we gradually come to know and trust over the years. Unlike the God about whom we are taught, and who lays on us the "shoulds" and "oughts" of a religious system, the God within—the Ground of our Being, as Tillich speaks of him—is not One in whom we *believe* as though he is apart from us and *about* whom we must speak. The Ground of our Being is One whom we *know* intimately.

Carl Jung was regarded by many as an agnostic because of his unorthodox views. In the latter years of his life he was asked if he believed in God. "No," Jung replied, "I don't believe in God, I know God!" To know God is to know within ourselves the Author of our life and the Authority before whom we must finally stand to render an accounting for what was done with it. It is my thesis that such a God is difficult to know, much less trust, before the mid-life crisis. Before this, external belief systems, a set of values, and/or cultural morals are believed by us to be authoritative. The God of Being is over forty and grows increasingly restless with our "nursery" needs for the Law. God longs for the day when we can dance with him in freedom and trust. It is a dance of joy and life. It is the God who is over forty who instigates the mid-life identity crisis because, like birth, it delivers us from the necessary but confining womb of religious institutionalism, with its necessary but tethering umbilical cord. It is a crisis of birth. Because of it we are pushed into the joy, freedom, and anxiety of New Life. Like birth, this crisis is accompanied by labor pains. We long for the security and warmth of another's protective body. But like birth, the delivery can be the beginning of the exhilarating adventure of independent life. The mid-life crisis is, in short, a chance to dance with the God of Grace.

It is important, or at least it was for me, to understand the mid-life crisis from a biblical-theological perspective. Strange things happen at such a time. Black becomes white, and right becomes wrong. Good becomes bad, and truth becomes error. There are a number of books available to help in understanding this topsy-turvy world from a psychological and sociological perspective. The former helped me to understand *what* was happening to me; the latter, *that* it happens to many. But I needed to understand *why* it was happening. I needed to know that it had meaning or purpose. What was the theology of this experience?

Ironically, the Bible was where I found my help. It was from these stories and faith statements that the God of Grace beckoned. Speaking autobiographically, James Fowler tells of a similar discovery in early mid-life when reflecting on his own faith development.

> In theological seminary I learned methods of studying scripture that employed language study, source criticism, form criticism and text criticism . . .[But] not until I was in my thirties . . .did I begin to learn a method of working with scripture that breathed more of the spirit . . .[one which] did not require me to give up or negate my critical skills, but . . . did . . . relinquish initiative to the text. Instead of *my reading,* analyzing and extracting the meaning of a Biblical text . . . I began to learn how to let the text *read me* and to let it bring my needs and the Spirit's movements within me to consciousness.[2]

I say "ironically" I found my help in scripture because the Bible has become the bastion of moral law and rational religion. Yet it is just these scaffold structures—necessary in the early building of a life—that must be dismantled if the life is to be lived. How absurd it would be to erect a scaffold so that a house might be built and then, when the house is completed, to leave the scaffold in place, interfering with its use. Yet, this is precisely what so often happens with things religious. Labels and Law take on an authority and hence an existence independent of

13

their function. Religion is a scaffold necessary in the development of a life. But human beings were never meant to exist for the sake of religion. Over the objection of the Pharisees, Jesus made it plain that wholeness and the enjoyment of life were more important than keeping the Sabbath law. The Sabbath, he said, was made for us, not we for the Sabbath. God—the Ground of our Being—created us in his image as partners for the dance of life. There comes a time when the scaffold gets in the way of people who want to dance. Jesus did not call us to be religious but to be human: "I came that [you] may have life, and have it abundantly" (John 10:10).

To fulfill such a promise, however, the relativity of religion must be exposed. Jesus offended the power structure because his allegiance was to God, not to the state or the synagogue. The resistance of the scaffold to being exposed and its relativity revealed comes graphically into focus in the crucifixion of Jesus. Ironically, it was not the political authorities who cried for his blood. It was the religious establishment. We may conclude that authoritarian powers are reluctant to give up their control of our lives, even if they are religious powers. Indeed, religious powers are especially reluctant to have their relativity exposed.

The Resurrection, therefore, is God's commentary on religious authority. It demonstrates that the Law is not ultimate. Religious regulation is not the last word, and its efforts to limit and label are not final. In the last analysis, Jesus and his threatening lifestyle are vindicated. The Resurrection says "Yes" to life and "No" to religion. God insists that Grace is more fundamental than Law. The Resurrection is a fracturing of the old life, built as it is upon religious authority. The Resurrection does not flow out of the Crucifixion. It interrupts it and the tidy but deadly definitions that religious authority would write. As such, the Resurrection is a threat to all that preceded the cross and transforms it into something new and different, perhaps even unrecognizable.

This tranforming power of New Life is what the middle-age crisis is about. The crisis, like the cross, is God's way of bringing to an end the old life, with its accumulation of limitations and restricting definitions. The old authorities are challenged. They are no longer accepted just because they are there. The Bible calls us to take responsibility for our lives, to own them and to live them. There are no guarantees. As we leave the old certainties behind, we may make mistakes. Our blunders may affect others as well. But the alternative is to sit out the dance. Clearly, some opt out. Jesus lamented, "We piped to you, and you did not dance . . ." (Matt. 11:17). But the melody lingers on. And to those who would respond, the Resurrection is the power of New Life beckoning to us, urging us, pushing us to risk dancing. The risk is that we may be changed. We may be altered in such a way that we are no longer recognized by our friends. Indeed, we may not recognize the strange new person in the bathroom mirror.

But there is no shortcut to this resurrection. We go by way of the cross, or we do not go at all. The Bible reminds us that the cross is the doorway to New Life. The mid-life crisis is just such a cross and, therefore, just such a doorway. Jesus' invitation to take up our cross and follow is, therefore, in fact good news. His cross is not a burden to be borne, nobly or otherwise, and his words are not a command of obedience. Rather, they are an invitation to open the door and to come dance with the God of Grace in that crazy world that the Bible calls the kingdom of God.

This, then, is not a book about a minister caught in the throes of middle age. Its concern is not voyeurism. It is rather a book that seeks to share some biblical-theological resources for those who see themselves as religious people but who find the needs, urges, and changes of middle age so perplexing that they wonder what is happening to them. Am I losing my faith, or worse, am I losing my mind? It is, to use again D.T. Niles' helpful analogy, one beggar telling another beggar where to find food.

The value of scripture, we will discover, is that it represents a story greater than our own. It helps us interpret our individual experience by sharing with us the larger experience of the people of God as they encountered life. Their stories and faith statements enlarge our understanding of what relationship with God means as we make the pilgrimage from cradle to grave, and all the times between. What I found in their accounts helped me to understand what was happening to me. It infused both the pain and the promise of middle age with an altogether unexpected perspective. It is to that understanding I want to bear witness.

Chapter One

The Crisis of Mid-Life

The Risk of Resurrection

As the autobiographical note of the Introduction indicates, my story is a tale of dying and rising, of endings and beginnings. As a theologian, I was a person dying of thirst. As a preacher, I felt burned out. I had nothing more to say. I had no more mountains to climb, no more dreams to share. I was a person who, as Gail Sheehy recognizes in her book *Passages,* was well into the mid-life crisis.

This identity crisis typically hits most of us between the ages of thirty-five and forty-five. It is characterized by restlessness. We are no longer sure of who we are, where we are going, or what we want to do.

You can imagine, then, that one of the details that caught my attention in a healing story recorded in the Gospels was the man's age. He was at least thirty-eight years old, and probably right in the middle of his own mid-life crisis.

Now there is in Jerusalem by the Sheep Gate a pool, in Hebrew called Bethzatha, which has five porticoes. In these lay a multitude of invalids, blind, lame, paralyzed. One man was there, who had been ill for thirty-eight years. When Jesus saw him and knew that he had been lying there a long time, he said to him, "Do you want to be healed?. . . Rise, take up your pallet, and walk." And at once the man was healed, and he took up his pallet and walked. (John 5:2-9)

The poor man was a charity case. Yet over the years he had managed to work out a certain routine for his life. He was an experienced beggar. Thirty-eight years of practice had made him an expert. He knew who he was. His identity was secure. He had come to terms with his handicap and knew what was expected of him. As a third-class citizen, he accepted the rules of the game and even found a certain satisfaction in successfully playing his prescribed part.

But then one day this Man of Grace walked into his life and everything changed. The cripple began to feel life flow again in his tired body. He began to sense a strange new vigor and strength. The old and familiar rules seemed arbitrary. The accustomed definitions no longer were adequate for the new person he was beginning to sense within himself. Dreams that had long been buried began to surface. The begging space was too confining, and the accustomed identity no longer fit. The Word of Life urged him to move on. Gail Sheehy generalizes his story and warns,

You can't take everything with you when you leave on the midlife journey. You are moving away. Away from institutional claims and other people's agenda. Away from external evaluations and accreditations, in search of an inner validation. You are moving out of roles and into the self. If I could give everyone a gift for the send-off on this journey, it would be a tent. A tent for tentativeness.[3]

If not a tent, at least a sleeping mat. Jesus told the man to take up his pallet and walk. The experience was such that the cripple spoke of being healed. Those who knew him agreed: He was a changed person.

The story of the biblical man is as contemporary as today's newspaper. One daily carried this story:

Ijmuiden, the Netherlands—A 60-year-old Dutch doctor, Kees den Hartoog, sailed yesterday into this North Sea port after a 264-day solo voyage around the world. He said that he had landed only once, last November, in Melbourne, and that he undertook the 30,000-mile voyage to realize a boyhood dream. He said that he would return to work within two weeks as a family doctor in the town of Broek.[4]

The newspaper reports the facts, but we have to read between the lines to get the whole story. A sixty-year-old man with his act together, an established physician in a community, highly respected, his practice rooted, his identity in place, one day begins to sense a dream, long buried, but unexpectedly and inconveniently coming to life. At first he dismisses the idea, denies its reality. But it persists. Gradually he realizes he can no longer deny it. Its urgency overwhelms him. Then one day it is clear: He has to leave his community and his practice, his family and his friends. He has to cut himself loose from the roles and the agendas that his old identity has laid on him. An old man is rejuvenated. He comes alive. His boyhood is resurrected. Off he goes to sail around the world by himself. His patients and family, no doubt, think he is crazy! At the very least: Irresponsible! Irrational! Immature!

The story is reported at least twelve times in the New Testament with variations. Each of the disciples, for whatever reason, followed Jesus because hanging out their sign "Business as usual" no longer fit. In each of them, Jesus touched a yearning nerve that awakened long-buried dreams and desires. They became restless. It meant having to leave behind families, their jobs, and the familiar roles that identified them in order to follow after this Man of Grace, but they sensed the promise of New Life.

So in our story, the man took up his pallet and began to move on. It would be nice if the story could end there, but unfortunately it cannot. Our friend encountered the criticism of the religious authorities who said, "What has happened is a terrible thing." The morality of the community had been offended. The lawmakers could see only the disruption of their tidy system. So the authorities told the man who had been healed:

> "This is a Sabbath, and it is against our Law for you to carry your mat." . . . So they began to persecute Jesus, because he had done this healing on a Sabbath. (John 5:10b, 16, TEV)

Resurrections are disruptive to the powers of death. When Igor Stravinsky's *Rite of Spring* was first performed, it caused a riot in the audience. The music is not predictably harmonious nor can it be called "pretty." The work represents Stravinsky's understanding of dormant life bursting forth in springtime. The music is itself an eruption of life, exploding unpredictably in the score. The themes are independent and often bear little relationship to one another. Pulsating with restlessness, they emerge urgently, powerfully, insistently. At times the music seems outright cacophonic, absurd, irrational, noisy, even brassy. But all of the apparent irrelevant themes, all of the competing sounds are written and directed into a symphonic portrayal of vibrant new life shattering death. Because the music does not develop according to our expectations, it is offensive. Because it is not predictable, we can never settle back comfortably and listen as though we know what is coming next. The outcome cannot be assumed. The discomfort caused a riot among the first listeners.

New Life is that way. It is seldom harmonious with the past. It erupts rather than flows forth logically or sequentially. Resurrections tend to upset the status quo and threaten the powers of Death.

James Fowler puts this religious truth in developmental terms:

> Restless with the self-images and outlook maintained by [one's religious development], the person ready for transition finds him- or herself attending to what may feel like anarchic and disturbing inner voices. Elements from a childish past, images and energies from a deeper self, a gnawing sense of the sterility and flatness of the meanings one serves—any or all of these may signal readiness for something new.[5]

But as Dostoevsky reminds us, "Taking a new step, uttering a new word, is what people fear most."

The call of life to those of us who are dead can be frightening. It is the threat of risking the new. While there is a certain comfort and security in being dead, life is uncertain and exciting. Sometimes too exciting. There is a sameness about death, and hence a predictability to it that makes it boring. The adventure of moving into an uncertain future, on the other hand, can be threatening because there are no guarantees. That time for many of us comes at mid-life. But we are afraid of resurrections because they are risky. We find New Life frightening. We are amazed at the recklessness of resurrected life. We may make mistakes, choose unwisely, or hurt loved ones.

Yet whatever the risks, in every one of us there are those faint stirrings of springtime, those urgings of resurrection that defy the cold clutch of death, the rigid but familiar patterns of existence, the safe but stifling roles that define us. These are the Easter urgings that erupt illogically, unexpectedly, in us. They represent the voice of life calling. They are the invitation to dance with God the Easter doxology.

I once listened to a mother tell the story of her daughter who died of cancer. Though the girl's body ultimately succumbed to the disease, her spirit never yielded. The story moved both of us to tears. The daughter's beauty and courage were eloquent affirmations that life is stronger than death. Death does not have the power to define us. Life in all of its manifestations is stronger than death in all of its disguises. Love is stronger than fear. Freedom is more contagious than enslavement. Giving is more appealing than taking. Gentleness is more persuasive than violence. There is in all of us the power of New Being, the pulsing power of life. Like springtime sap, which begins to flow in the trees, there is a life energy that heals us when we are sick or injured. It revitalizes us when we despair. It affirms us when we feel down and defeated, and it carries us through that curtain that we call death into new life.

Howard Thurman likened that power to an underground river that flows in us, unknown and perhaps unrecognized, but there nevertheless. In the crisis of mid-life it emerges. It surfaces with power and promise. We sense its energy when we are in love and feel alive. We sense its flow when we are excited and are caught up in a great cause that demands of us our best. We sense it in the satisfaction of a job well done. Tillich says we sense ultimacy in the common, ordinary things of life, unexpectedly, unexplainably; but it is there and sometimes it emerges. And when it does, in that instant, we know we are alive. When we yield ourselves to the current within and allow it to carry us along, we *live*. In so doing, we do God's will, for she wills life.

A friend of mine starts every day with three words. When he gets up in the morning, he says, "I am." And then he adds, "Yes." Obedience to God is to affirm ourselves by saying *yes* to life. It is saying *yes* to our lives and whatever the day may bring. It is saying *yes* to those wellsprings that emerge within each of us. It is saying *yes* to the call or the nudge within. Mary Richards contends that we must trust these feelings:

We have to trust the invisible gauges we carry within us. We have to realize that a creative being lives within ourselves, whether we like it or not, and that we must get out of its way, for it will give us no peace until we do.[6]

But these resurrections are risky and entrusting ourselves to the currents of New Life may be frightening, not only because others may not recognize us but because we may not even recognize ourselves.

There is an interesting and disturbing detail in two of the accounts concerning Jesus' resurrection. In John's account, Mary Magdalene went to the tomb early while it was still dark and discovered the tomb to be empty. But when she turned around and saw the risen Christ, she did not recognize him. John says, "She turned round and saw Jesus standing, but she *did not know that it was Jesus*" (Italics added—John 20:14). In Luke's story of the Resurrection the disciples were walking along the road to Emmaus. "While they were talking and discussing together, Jesus himself drew near and went with them. *But their eyes were kept from recognizing him.*" (Italics added—Luke 24:15-16.) Jesus was different after the Resurrection. Whatever else we may say about the Resurrection, it is clear from these two accounts that it changed Jesus in such a way that even his closest friends and associates no longer recognized him. Clearly, when the New Testament invites us to share in the New Life of Christ, there is a certain risk involved. We may become different persons.

So we are caught betwixt and between. Fearful, yet restless. Impatient, yet imprisoned in old roles and expectations. Frustrated with the old being but unsure of the new.

Nevertheless, the last word is resurrection! The power of life is more resilient than that of death. Risky or not, resurrection prevails. The flow of life moves on. Grace transcends Law. In spite of our inner confusion and despite all of the misgivings about who we are, the broken selves of our being are like a beaten army fleeing in disorder from victory already achieved. Christ is Lord, and life wills its way in us. The mid-life crisis opens the door to the great adventure of New Life. Its advent is, therefore, frightfully good news.

The Great Adventure: Focus on Joseph

Curiously, the forces which drive a person into the great adventure of mid-life and beyond are frequently mobilized by some disruptive trauma. It may be the loss of a job, the death of a loved one, a move to a new location, the breakup of a marriage, or the graying of hair. It may be a major occurrence or an insignificant event. For Joseph of the Gospels it was the discovery that his fiancée was pregnant.

21

It is interesting how the various writers handle the event. Luke, for example, is concerned with Mary, while Matthew is fascinated by Joseph. The difference is instructive. Traditionally, Mary is the one who gets the play especially at Christmas time. All of the attention is on the lovely young Madonna and the bambino. Joseph, if we think of him at all, stands in the background. We imagine him as at least middle aged; rather colorless and conservative, but steady and dependable. Above all, sensible and rational.

For Mary, the conception of Jesus was a matter of unusual concern. But it is also clear from Luke's account that trusting came easily for Mary. After an initial period of some uneasiness, she accepted the fact without great questioning and was able to say to the angel, "Behold, I am the handmaid of the Lord; let it be to me according to your word" (Luke 1:38).

For Joseph, however, the conception of Jesus was a major trauma. It nearly blew the poor man out of the water! Let us look at Matthew's version.

Now the birth of Jesus Christ took place in this way. When his mother Mary had been betrothed to Joseph, before they came together she was found to be with child of the Holy Spirit; and her husband Joseph, being a just man and unwilling to put her to shame, resolved to divorce her quietly. But as he considered this, behold, an angel of the Lord appeared to him in a dream, saying, "Joseph, son of David, do not fear to take Mary your wife, for that which is conceived in her is of the Holy Spirit; she will bear a son, and you shall call his name Jesus, for he will save his people from their sins." . . . When Joseph woke from sleep, he did as the angel of the Lord commanded him; he took his wife, but knew her not until she had borne a son; and he called his name Jesus. (Matt. 1:18-25)

Joseph discovered, long before Sam Keen did, that the Holy Spirit is a wild dove, not a tame pigeon. For middle-aged, rational Joseph, steeped in conventional morality, and knowledgeable in religious law, Mary's pregnancy was a fracturing experience. It totally destroyed his world. It was obvious to Joseph that Mary, his betrothed, was pregnant. It was equally clear to him that he was not the father. The conclusion was inescapable: She had been fooling around. By any moral or religious standard, such behavior was inexcusable. But Joseph was a rational man. He did not respond to the situation emotionally. He did not get a gun and shoot her. No, he did the sane, mature thing. He decided to put her away quietly, to divorce her without any ruckus. Middle age has its own kind of wisdom and that would be a just and moral way to handle the sordid affair.

Joseph is to be commended. After all, Mary's account of it comes up lame. Imagine, for example, a high school girl announcing to her church school class, "I am pregnant, and it is by the Holy Spirit." No one would probably burst out laughing. Church people are too polite for that, but neither would anyone buy her story. So Joseph's conclusion is understandable, and his intention laudable.

Nevertheless, in the middle of his mid-life crisis, Joseph has a change of mind. He sees things differently. As in a conversion experience, what seemed so obvious is now not clear at all, and what was unthinkable becomes imperative: Joseph takes Mary as his wife—pregnancy and all.

Matthew invites us to see that in these scandalous events— these fracturing, disruptive, world-shaking events for Joseph— the Holy Spirit was calling Joseph to trust God rather than convention. I mean Trust with a capital T. I am talking about Trust that means an entire change of lifestyle. Rudolph Otto, in describing the confrontation with the Holy, speaks of the Holy breaking into and destroying our human categories of under-standing and shattering the nice coherencies that we have managed to make. To encounter God is to have our common sense, our morality, our rationality fractured. Can you imagine what Joseph's cronies must have thought of his change of plans? All of them God-fearing, church-attending, law-abiding, Bible-reading, religious people—champions of God, motherhood, and country. They could only shake their heads at Joseph and whisper behind his back. "How Joseph has changed! I could support him when he wouldn't have anything to do with a woman like that. He used to have his head on straight. He was sensible when he was thinking about leaving her. But now, look at him! He's embracing her and endorsing her behavior. He's even buying her story and thinking of this pregnancy as an act of God. He's senile, I fear. Joseph has changed for the worse. What a shame!" Trust for Mary was as natural as breathing. But trust for Joseph was the death of a world view and the birth of a whole new way of understanding life.

When we first meet Joseph in the story, he reminds us of the American ideal, the epitome of cool control: sane, rational, analytical, unemotional, in charge of the situation, and steady as a rock. Our educational system trains us, and our culture encourages us, to raise questions, analyze problems, and seek solutions. We are urged to set goals, and success is measured by our ability to achieve them. In a technological society we need to manipulate our environment and control the variables. We have to be in charge of our lives and our destiny. Sam Keen speaks of this neurotic need to be in control as the great American sin:

> One symptom of the American way of sin, we're told, is that a third to one-half of Americans suffer from constipation and hemorrhoids. We are also told that salvation from this sin is Preparation H. It is typical of the American character that we believe in scientific nostrums. In reality, constipation and hemor-rhoids are philosophical problems that science and medicine cannot solve. From childhood we are told that we must control ourselves. The head must control the body. The body must function regularly and follow orders. It must eliminate wastes once every twelve hours. To comply with our constipated need for control and order, to do our duty regularly, we push until the pushing is translated into hemorrhoids. This is the model of unfaith, of untrust. Hemorrhoids, the national disease, is the sign of our paranoia or, in theological terms, of our untrust.[7]

Joseph, like so many of us, was constipated—if not physically, then emotionally, spiritually. Nothing could be admitted into his frame of reference that did not fit or over which he had no control. Then God called to middle-aged Joseph. In these scandalous events God was nudging Joseph to let go of his wisdom and trust God's foolishness, to let go of his morality and trust a dream that came to him in the middle of the night. In these painful and unplanned events, God was inviting Joseph to trust her and cut loose from all the conventional anchors which gave stability and security to Joseph, but which also weighed him down and held him back. Joseph was to discover that authentic life involves being broken open and remaining porous to the amazing intrusions of Reality. To trust God meant accepting the intrusion of Mary's pregnancy as a gift of grace.

By focusing on Joseph, Matthew has invited us to look at the absurd disruptions of our sane lives and find there the God of Grace who, with what at times appears to be demented humor, invites us to dance with her. Such disruptions are opportunities provided by God which move us from anchored life to trusting life. Because they have power to transform us they are to be seen as miraculous events, and the mid-life time seems to have more than its share of them. Unfortunately we often do not recognize these miracles when they occur, and usually speak of them disparagingly. Elizabeth Barrett Browning, however, reminds us that,

> Earth's crammed with heaven
> And every common bush aflame with God.
> And only he who sees takes off his shoes
> The rest sit round it and pluck blackberries.[8]

The same can be said of the mid-life period. It is crammed with miracle signs of the time, grace time, but only those who see take off their shoes. The rest sit round and lament the fact that the times—they are a-changing.

Signs of the Time

Let us for a bit look more closely at these miracle signs in order to see just what they are and how they function in our lives. When speaking of angels, Karl Barth once observed we need a sense of humor. Unfortunately, when we speak of miracles, modern Americans have an overdeveloped sense of humor; it is difficult for us to take them seriously. None but the most literal minded considers their occurrence a possibility. Rather, we dismiss them as supernatural peculiarities that no longer happen or happen with such infrequency that a second thought is not merited. There is no place for them in a closed-ended, cause-and-effect world view. Something occurred that had a very natural explanation, unknown to the people of biblical times. Therefore, it was called an act of God, and the label "miracle" was attached to it.

It is difficult in a technological, scientific age to give serious credence to a discussion of miracles. It is interesting, therefore, that the Gospel of John does not even use the word. John never talks about "miracles." Instead, he speaks of "signs." For John, miracles were signs that God had enfleshed herself in Jesus. The situation John was facing as a theologian and writer was that he had to present Jesus to his readers as more than simply a Jewish prophet, an itinerant faith healer, or another Greek savior figure. John's concern was to show Jesus as nothing less than the eternal Word of God become flesh. Therefore, these spectacular happenings, or miracles, John called "signs." They pointed to the fact that Jesus is no less than the eternal Logos of God become flesh.

Unfortunately, John's concern is not a burning issue among most Christians today. Therefore, the question to which he addressed himself might more profitably be asked, "What sort of God is this who has enfleshed herself in Jesus? What do these signs tell us about God?" Here, of course, we have several possibilities from which to draw, none of which are entirely satisfying.

One way of viewing miracles is to see them as signs of God's love and concern for us. God, who is interested in our well-being, performs miracles such as causing the lame to walk, the deaf to hear, the blind to see. These indicate God's intention that we be whole and healthy persons.

Certainly healing miracles are signs of God's love and concern, but miracles are not needed to make the point. Any analysis of the life forces within us will do the same. Doctors, for example, tell us that they do not cause healing to take place. The body heals itself. The doctor can only facilitate the process. The healing power, the life force or energy to live resides in the body, not with whatever the doctor may do. One study of mental illness was particularly instructive because it indicated statistically that whether or not the doctor or psychiatrist intervened was irrelevant to the healing of the person mentally ill. The mere passage of time did as well. Miracles, therefore, are not needed as signs to indicate God's concern and love for us. We can discover it for ourselves by simply looking at the life force within us.

Another way of viewing miracles is to see them as signs of God's power. Again true! But, again, there is nothing new in that. Any self-respecting god would have the muscle to do amazing things. It goes with the job. To point, therefore, to the calming of the storm, or the raising of the dead, as a display of divine power is certainly true, but trite. It is not news nor do we need a miracle to tell us God is great. We could have guessed as much for ourselves.

One of the most self-serving interpretations of miracles is to see them as signs of divine favor. This is how some evangelists often interpret them—particularly, evangelists of the radio and television variety. The pitch goes something like this; "God is doing wondrous things out there in radio land. This past week I received letters from 400 (or 4000) of my listeners reporting miraculous things happening. See how God is working through my radio ministry. Therefore, to keep this marvelous work going, send your checks to me in care of the station to which you are listening." Miracles become the proof that the evangelist's efforts are worth supporting, and the more miracles the evangelist can claim, the more justification for reaching into our pockets. God loves a cheerful giver and the miracles proved she has a special love for the givee.

We could, of course, look at other interpretations but they would bring us no closer to answering the question, "What news do these signs tell us concerning God?" So let us go back to square one. Let us begin again by asking a very simple question. What, functionally speaking, is a miracle? That is to say, what does a miracle do? If we look at all the reported miracles in the Bible, what is the common denominator?

The answer is disarmingly simple. The one thing they all have in common is they are *intrusions* into the normal expectations of things.

The Cana wedding celebration is in danger of falling flat because the wine has run out. The party will be a real bust and there is nothing to do but make the best of it. That would be our normal expectation. Then Jesus intrudes and turns water into wine. (Cf. John 2:1-10.)

Lazarus dies and the crowd gathers for the funeral service. There is much weeping and mourning. What else would you expect when burying the dead? But then Jesus enters the scene and breaks up the funeral by bringing the deceased back to life. (Cf. John 11:1-44.)

The disciples have been out in the boat fishing all night. Their luck has been terrible. No fish! Gloomily they row back toward shore until Jesus enters the picture and says, "Cast your nets on the other side of the boat." There are now so many fish the nets break. (Cf. John 21:4-8.)

Miracles are intrusions into the normal expectation of things. Miracles, therefore, are signs that our God likes *surprises*. Life takes on a certain routine, predictable in nature, but dull in its continuance. And then God decides to touch our life. Something happens. Surprise! The normal expectations are interrupted. God intrudes into the status quo with *new possibilities* that boggle the mind. She reveals new avenues we never dreamed were there. Old categories we thought had been closed are reopened. The definitions we thought had been settled—of possible and impossible, right and wrong, good and bad—now have to be rethought.

The Saturday Evening Post told the story of Dr. Anthony Sattilaro, president of Philadelphia's Methodist Hospital. Riddled by cancer, in his spinal column, the brain, and throughout his body, he was given, at most, eighteen months to live. Out of desperation, he tried what is called a macrobiotic diet that consisted largely of grains and natural foods. The article that, according to all available tests, Dr. Sattilaro was completely cured. His healing was called a miracle.[9]

But his healing was *not* the miracle. Perhaps in fifty or one hundred years we shall better understand macrobiotics and the relationship of natural foods to the healing processes of the body. Then we will see the natural connection between diet and cancer and not think of calling such a healing a miracle. What then was the miracle?

The miracle is tucked away in the story of how Dr. Sattilaro came to *learn* about macrobiotics. He was returning from the funeral of his father, fully mindful of death all around him, including his own. On a whim he did something he normally would never do: He picked up two hitchhikers. Furthermore, the usual polite conversation took an unusual twist. "How are you?" "Well, I'm dying of cancer. How are you?" One of the hitchhikers said, "You don't need to die of cancer. Haven't you ever heard of macrobiotics?" The doctor was in no mood to be instructed in the practice of medicine by a hitchhiker, but a couple days later he received in the mail a book from his hitchhiker friend—with postage due. He read the book, visited some of the places talked about, and phoned some of the people mentioned in the book. He was convinced enough—or desperate enough—to try the program. As a result, Anthony Sattilaro got well. Where was the miracle? It was the interruption in the normal routine of a doctor who had all of the medical answers, all of which were quite useless. It began with a whim to pick up two hitchhikers: something he would never ordinarily do.

In an earlier book, *God Our Loving Enemy* (Abingdon, 1982), I shared the experience of my loss of voice and the crisis it brought to my preaching career. After four and a half years I received my voice back because of surgery performed in San Francisco. In the book I called it a miracle. But it was not a miracle. It was just excellent surgery. The miracle was the *loss* of my voice. It was the interruption in my career and the dislocation of my self-esteem. The depression that followed my loss of voice made me do business with myself and discover my true worth as an individual. The miracle was that I came to like myself, croaky voice and all. Long before surgery became a possibility, I was able to say, "Though I would never choose to lose my voice, I would not trade the experience for anything in the world." That was the miracle.

It is important, therefore, to note what characterizes miracles, lest we miss them. Miracles are almost never supernatural events. They may be, but they almost never are—that is why we miss so many of them. We notice only the spectacular ones without natural causal explanation, and these are few indeed. But it is the quality of interruption in the usual that characterizes a miracle. It appears unexpectedly in the normal run of things. The disruption in the normal routine of our life may be natural or supernatural, but it is the quality of *intrusion* that typifies the presence of a miracle. Often miracles are inconveniences. Usually they are unwanted. At times they may even appear to be outrageous. But that is how we know them as signs: signs that God is touching our life. She is bored with the routine and is saying to us, "Ford may have a good idea, but I have a better one. Surprise!"

The children leave home, an illness overtakes us, we find ourselves falling in love, a transfer to a new job comes our way. Miracles are nothing more nor less than the interruptions in the routine that alter our perception of life *gracefully*. They are signs of the time—Grace time. Time for us to grow again and to have our vision enlarged. Time for our eyes to be opened, and our ears unstopped, our hands and our feet unshackled so that we might follow the restless God who calls us to join her on the dance floor where life is seen differently. Mid-life is typically a time of such surprises. It is a time for miracles. And, therefore, it is a time of turbulence.

Trusting the Turbulence

Turbulence, of course, is not unique to middle age. Indeed, experience leads us to conclude that to be a Christian is to be condemned to a life of turbulence. There are many ominous storm warnings scattered throughout the Bible. Jesus, for example, says, "I have not come to bring peace, but a sword" (Matt. 10:34). Even more cryptically, he tells us to take up our cross and follow him. Dietrich Bonhoeffer caught the point and observed that when Jesus calls a person to discipleship, he bids that person come and die. Yet the great discovery of the mid-life journey is that the death we are required to undergo has a broader meaning than physical death. It involves the death of confidence in external authorities—especially religious authorities—and daring to trust the God within. This is experienced as New Life, but as we have noted earlier, there is no shortcut to such resurrection. It is great to mount up with wings like eagles, as Isaiah says (Isa. 40:31). But the author of Deuteronomy reminds us that in order for us to soar, God, like a mother eagle, insists on stirring up the nest (Deut. 32:11). Life is often like the experience of flying in a plane when the cabin light comes on warning us to fasten our seat belts. The voice of the captain comes over the speaker and announces, "We expect to encounter a little turbulence." The difference is that when God makes the announcement it usually is an understatement. To be visited by God is to encounter turbulence. Much of it. She stirs up the nest of our lives, and the question is, "How are we to understand the turbulence so that we can indeed trust it?"

It would seem that God's intention is to break us open so we may be porous to new possibilities. There is a song occasionally sung in churches that has very peculiar words:

> Spirit of the living God, fall afresh on me;
> Spirit of the living God, fall afresh on me.
> *Break me,* melt me, mold me, fill me.
> Spirit of the living God, fall afresh on me.[10]

The words often slip by us unnoticed because the melody is so lovely. We enjoy singing it. But when we stop to consider the words, they seem to concur with an observation once made by Sam Keen, "The sanctuary [of the Lord] is always on shaky ground. God loves earthquakes."[11] God wills to break open the status quo of our lives. She desires to disrupt our routine. Thomas Kelly in his classic *A Testament of Devotion* laments:

> It is an overwhelming experience to fall into the hands of the living God, to be invaded to the depths of one's being by His presence, to be, without warning, wholly uprooted from all earthborn securities and assurances, and to be blown by a tempest of unbelievable power which leaves one's old proud self utterly, utterly defenseless, until one cries, "all thy waves and thy billows are gone over me." (Ps. 42:7)[12]

It is this uprooting, this fracturing, this tearing away from the familiar and being broken open to the new which is so painful, and this is the reason why suffering is a part of being human. Unfortunately, pain has gotten a bad press in our society. Third World nations, because they are not the beneficiaries of advanced medical technology, have learned the lessons of pain. We, on the other hand, seek to avoid them. If we hurt, we take an aspirin or a tranquilizer, or go on a vacation, or get drunk. No one likes to hurt. But the fact of the matter is that pain helps the doctor locate the problem. Pain has value.

So, too, does the pain of turbulence. Pain can make us angry, and anger can motivate us to act, to break out of some bondage. Pain can cause us to question the neat, tidy fantasies by which we live, which bear no relationship to the realities of life. Pain can relocate our commitments and priorities. Such new possibilities are only viable when the old has been destroyed and we have been broken open. God stirs the nest of our lives and creates turbulence as her way of cutting us loose from all of the comfortable security that can suffocate us. When things are no longer nailed down in our lives, change is possible.

It follows, therefore, that turbulence makes growth possible. The young eagles are comfortable in their nest. They have a good life. The mother bird brings the prey to the nest so the fledglings need do nothing. Then one day, in the name of maturity and growth, the mother eagle stirs the nest and the little fledglings complain, "Hey, be careful. It's a long way down.

We could get hurt." But the mother smiles lovingly and says in the language of eagles, "I know," and pushes them out. God stirs up the nest of our lives because her concern is not with our comfort, but with our maturity and growth. She wants us to realize all the potential that is in us and catch the vision of making a miracle of our lives. We only pass this way once and God wants us to make the most of the opportunity.

When we realize we are standing on an ice floe that is breaking up, we are motivated to act. We jump to one side or the other. It is clear we must move on. Similarly, when in middle age our perceptions of things are altered and we begin to see that the old myths by which we have been living no longer fit, or that familiar labels no longer apply, we then have the possibility of seeing the *new*. As the apostle Paul pointed out, when the old has passed away, the new can come (2 Cor. 5:17).

The question is, of course, "How can we be sure that the breakup of the familiar, the turbulence that comes upon us, is in fact meant for our well-being and growth?" The answer is of course we cannot—not in advance. Certainty only comes when we look over our shoulder and can trace the straight line of God's guidance through the crooked paths of our experience. But our next step always has to be taken in faith. We walk by faith, not by sight. Yet the central assertion of our faith is that God is like a parent. In the midst of all life's turbulence, those simple words proclaim the most important assertion we can make about life, for they make answers unimportant. They hover over all of our existence and justify every delay. They illuminate the darkness. Whoever believes them is able to walk in the light, and whoever does not believe them lives in darkness. Whoever hopes in those words can rejoice, but whoever does not hope in them is still in anguish. Whoever loves those words has life. Whoever does not love those words is overshadowed by death. God is our Parent.

The point is simply that, if God is our Parent, we shall not attribute the events of our life, and certainly not its turbulence, to chance. We shall consider them as signs of God's parental love. And this holds true for the ultimate turbulence, the final disrupter of life, namely death. Instinctively we fear death as the ultimate insult to our being. Understandably we seek to deny the fear or displace it. Keen confesses, autobiographically:

One of my favorite strategies for avoiding [death] is to focus on the fear that my woman will abandon me. [It places] the mask of the unthinkable terror over the living face of the one I love.[13]

We might add, parenthetically, that we surround marriage with vows, trying to nail down the relationship and thereby guarantee its stability. We seek to avoid the inevitable unfaithfulness of separation: being deserted for another suitor—Death. I remember a funeral I once had. The elderly husband had died. The grieving widow stood by the grave crying pathetically, "Addison, you promised. You promised you wouldn't leave me." Addison was unfaithful to his promise.

Keen continues:

How can I accept Death without dying? How can I touch without grasping, love without placing the expectations of permanency upon the loved one? If I could learn that nothing could save me I might stop looking for a savior.[14]

This is the human predicament. We desperately look for saviors who can deliver us from the turbulence. But God—like a loving mother eagle—insists upon stirring up the nest. In the end she brings on death, the final turbulence. It is the growth spurt that casts us into what the Gospel of John calls, "eternal life."

Carlo Carreto, in a book of meditations, sees the disruption of death as a part of life's larger purpose and therefore welcomes this final stirring of the nest.

Come then, death!
Come, I am waiting.
You do not frighten me any more.
I no longer see you as my foe.
I see you as a sister.
I look you in the face.
I understand you now.
And as you come towards me, I tell you thinking of him who holds you firmly in his mighty hand, *"Do with me what you will."*
Wholeheartedly I say this to you.
Truthfully I say this to you.
Lovingly I say this to you:
"Do with me what you will."
Accustom me to this extreme abandonment . . .
Accustom me little by little, by distributing my death through all the days of my life.

Put it on my bread like ashes or sand, so that I do *"not live by bread alone."* (Cf. Matt. 4:4.)

Put it in my house as *"something lacking,"* so that I do not accept the limitations of the visible.

Put it as insecurity into my security, so that I may only be secure in Him who is the Absolute.[15]

God uses death and all of the little distributions of death sprinkled throughout our life, which constitute its turbulence, to teach us that we stand before her alone. Turbulence, therefore, reminds us of our solitude. We may not always realize the fact of our aloneness. Indeed, we usually resist facing it. We run from the truth by surrounding ourselves with companions and activities so that the truth is insulated from us. But if the point is missed earlier, it cannot be escaped at death. Our aloneness is the truth of our existence. Nobody can do our living for us. Nobody can do our dying for us. No one else can take responsibility for what we do with our lives. They are ours and were entrusted to no one else. We alone are held accountable for them before God.

Maturity brings its own kind of wisdom; I now understand and appreciate better than I once did the monastic movement. I used to think that the desire to enter a monastery was an attempt to escape from life. Mind you, I am still not big on the vows of poverty and chastity, but I think I understand now why persons who are disturbed or troubled might go to a monastery. It is not because they are escaping from life. It is because they have come to realize the great truth of life. They are alone. And they enter a monastery because they need to learn the lessons of solitude. Jeremiah explained, "I sat alone, because thy hand was upon me" (Jer. 15:17).

The cry of Jesus on the cross "My God, my God, why?" is instinctive in all of us. We know that life boils down to the two of us: "You and me, Lord." It was said during World War II that there were no atheists in foxholes. This is simply another way of saying that, when the supports are pulled away, when loved ones are separated from us, when the traditional answers no longer make sense, we realize as did Jesus—we are alone before God. It is a universal recognition. "The challenge of death comes to us all and no one can die for another," said Luther. "Everyone must fight his own battle with death by himself, alone . . . I will not be with you then, nor you with me."

The Bible speaks of God as a jealous God. She is our Lover, and she will not settle for anything or anyone else being central in our lives. She removes any competition. The turbulence reminds us of this fact. Until we learn the lesson that God is the great Lover of the universe, the great Companion with whom life is to be danced, the One in whom we must ultimately find our strength and joy—until we learn that lesson, the disturbances come. For in the disturbances we realize the inadequacies of all other loves and lovers. When we are stripped and broken open, God speaks to us. It is in the aloneness we come to realize the truth in Jonathan Edwards' observation that, in the last analysis, a person's business is with God. The message becomes increasingly clear in the turbulence of middle age.

Chapter Two
Pulling Up Roots and Moving On

The Restlessness of God

The fortieth birthday is a significant, if not always traumatic, event. It is a turning point: the end of young adulthood and the beginning of middle age. It is, therefore, interesting that the big four O is also a significant time from a biblical perspective. For example, not until forty years of turbulent wandering in the wilderness had elapsed did God feel Israel was ready to move into the land of promise. Those forty years were a time of transition from the old to the new. That amount of time was necessary as a preparation for what was yet to come. There was no avoiding them or hurrying them along.

Furthermore, those years of wilderness wandering were formative for Israel's faith. Her earliest understanding of God was that he was not one who resided in a building with foundations made of concrete sunk deep in the earth to withstand the winds of change. Rather the Lion of Judah was One who dwelt in a tabernacle or tent, the stakes of which could be pulled up at a moment's notice and moved whenever he had the whim to travel. God's presence was symbolized for Israel by a pillar of fire by night and a column of smoke by day. Whenever it moved, the whole community of faith had to follow or be left behind. After forty years of life with Father in the wilderness, Israel was convinced her covenant partner was a restless God who kept on the move.

The Wanderer is the God of Grace, and the restlessness of middle age signifies that he is near at hand. We know he is near when we feel the heavy footsteps of his presence shaking the foundations of our lives. We recognize his advent when we, like Job, are overcome by the whirlwind of life. All of the well thought out answers that once made sense are now rendered inadequate. A mockery is made of the advice that friends and comforters offer, based on an accepted morality and a conventional wisdom in which God has absolutely no interest. Just when we get our faith worked out so that God makes some sense, just when we begin to understand how things fit together and we can begin to lay plans, thinking we know how life will unfold— just then the winds of the spirit hit us like a tornado and all of our preconceptions crumble. Just when we get our value system put in place and know right from wrong, good from evil, just then God breaks into our lives and shatters everything that we held sacred. Just when we get our careers organized so that we can begin to look ahead and set goals, just then God—like a whirlwind—scatters all of the blueprints. In short, the God of Grace is:

> like a child, who dares to inquire beyond the limits of conventional answers. He discovers the fragmentary character of all these answers, a character darkly and subconsciously felt by all men. He may destroy, by means of one fundamental question, a whole, well-organized system of life and society, of ethics and religion. He may show that what people believed to be a whole is nothing but a fragment of a fragment. He may shake the certainty on which centuries lived, by unearthing a riddle or an enigma in its very foundation.[16]

Like the little boy who was supposed to see the emperor dressed in fine new clothes, God steps into our social conventions, points his finger at all the things that we hold sacred, and says, "Look, there is nothing there! The emperor is absolutely naked."

Restlessness is a sign of God's presence. When life is touched by such a God, we have to move on because instinctively we know that to stay with the familiar and the conventional is to be left behind. Howard Thurman offers this analogy:

> An old mother duck brought her young ducklings down to what had once been a pond. Since her last brood of ducklings, the pond had become nothing but baked mud. But the mother did

not realize this. She stood on the bank urging the ducklings to go down, swim around, and disport themselves on the chickweed where there was no water and the chickweed had long since disappeared. While she was doing this, her ducklings with their fresh young instincts smelled the chickweed and heard the water way up above the dam. So they left their mother beside her old pond to go in quest of other water or get lost on the way (this is the risk). They said to her as they left, "Mother, for you and all the generations of your ducklings before us, this may have been good water. But if you and yours would swim again, it must be in other waters."[17]

In this moving on there is no intention to hurt nor be irreverent. Rather it is simply the response to the basic urge to live life. The God of Grace calls to us and nudges us on. Creator to creature. Image to image. Restlessness to restlessness.

But what is this wilderness that the God of Grace invites us to enter? What is the nature of this domain beyond the comfortable, secure, structured world governed by common sense and answers that can be systematized and understood? Some call it the Bad Lands. Others speak of it as the Desert. One fact is certain. It is No Person's Land. It is *God's* kingdom. It is a wilderness where no familiar landmarks will guide us because we must learn to trust only God. It is the abode where the restless God, the God of Grace wanders. It is a world of surprises and absurdities. It is a world spoken of as "unbelievable and fantastic." It is a world in which we pinch ourselves and exclaim "I must be dreaming. This can't be real." In 1970 Sam Keen began his book *To a Dancing God*—a sort of diary—with these words about his mid-life journey into the wilderness.

Once upon a time there was an unchanging God who was king over an orderly world in which change occurred so benevolently it was called progress. There was a place and a time for everything. Six days for work and one for being told the meaning of work. And certain things were not done on Sunday. There were authorities too. The minister and priest spoke without hesitation of God and his requirements. Dad and Mother told us what good boys and girls did (or mostly didn't do). The newspaper told it like it was. Uncle Sam could be trusted to make the world safe for democracy. And filling in all the cracks between constituted authorities were reason and common sense.

Then something happened. Some say God died. This much we know: everything that was nailed down suddenly came loose.

Chaos was king and the moral world looked like a furniture store after a hurricane. Everywhere the credentials of the authorities were challenged and great imposters were discovered in high circles.[18]

What Keen calls the king of chaos, however, is in fact the restless God of Grace stirring the nest. Lesslie Newbigin, world class theologian, calls this disturbance "The reign of God." Addressing a gathering of church leaders, Newbigin pondered the problem:

God reigns is the most tremendous item of world news that you can imagine...the fact that God reigns over all things is no longer something in another world . . . . if God cares to use us, we may be the place in which that miraculous supernatural work of the Spirit is done. But if it is done, it will change us as well as change the world . . . . The miracle of the Kingdom of God has broken in and *somebody has to try to explain it.*[19](italics added)

It is significant that when the disciples encountered the inbreaking power of the God of Grace at Pentecost, they went into the streets and tried to tell the world. But the world thought they were not only babbling idiots but stewed to the gills as well. Yet as Newbigin says, "Someone has to try to explain it." It is almost impossible to understand the explanation prior to our fortieth birthday. We are too busy nailing life down and securing our name and nest. Indeed, we are not at all sure we understand it afterward. But somehow, someone has to try to explain what happens when the restless God calls us to move on to the land of freedom and New Life.

Five years after Keen wrote *To a Dancing God,* he had left the familiar homeland and crossed the frontier into the new land: the wilderness, the No Person's Land called the kingdom of God. He tries to explain life in the new world in these words taken from a later book, *Beginnings Without End:*

One morning, just when it seemed the deadness of Winter would never pass, Person awoke unexpectedly to find green tendrils pushing up the lid of the Tomb of Nothingness. S/he felt the stirrings of New Life and decided to walk about and see what the World would look like now that the Old Authorities were dead.

Surprising things began to happen quite without Person's initiative or control. The New World seemed to reach out and welcome Person. Enchanted animals flocked around. Hawks and snakes came bearing Omens. There were dreams filled with messages, juicy as watermelons. Suddenly the World seemed to be a cypher, a hidden language of some Divine Presence, which Person knew made sense but could not quite understand. The Old World had been governed by Cause and Effect and other Laws written by the Society of Scientists, Moralists and Lawyers. But the New World was filled with Marvel and Synchronicity and as nearly as Person could determine seemed to be governed by a Council of Magicians, Comedians and Lovers.[20]

That is the world the God of Grace calls us to enter, a world which seems to be "governed by a Council of Magicians, Comedians and Lovers."

There are two temptations awaiting the pilgrim who would follow the Wanderer into the new land. The first is the temptation to go back into the old familiar world of safe, certain definitions. The Hebrews from their precarious freedom in the wilderness cried out to Moses, "Would that we had died by the hand of the Lord in the land of Egypt, when we sat by the fleshpots and ate bread to the full; for you have brought us out into this wilderness to kill this whole assembly with hunger" (Exod. 16:3). The fleshpots of Egypt were an attraction precisely because they offered security. Slavery was tempting because it was at least a known and predictable existence. Living by Grace is absurdly unpredictable. It is indicative that the Man of Grace, Jesus, was crucified by the steady, dependable bureaucracy, which he continually threatened. It was not that Jesus was antagonistic toward the established mores. Rather it was because he lived in a different world, a world in which the healing of a person was more important than honoring the value system that was commonly held. Jesus' life raises the questions for all of us: What if Grace is more fundamental than Law: What if Grace is more fundamental than our honored institutions such as church, government, or marriage? What if Grace is more fundamental than our orthodoxies? What if Grace is more fundamental than our morality? Such questions can be terribly unnerving and threatening. The temptation, therefore, is to turn our back on the new world and go back to the security and slavery of the old one.

The second temptation that awaits the pilgrim is the desire to freeze the moments of Grace. We desperately want to hold on to them, preserving them forever. Again, it is significant that in the story of the wandering in the wilderness, the God of

Grace provided food from heaven, manna, for each day's need. But there was no excess given. And the instructions that came with it prohibited trying to collect it or preserve it.

Moments of Grace are so beautiful and satisfying. We want to put them under glass and keep them forever. But like manna, they will not keep. Grace cannot be stored. Moments of Grace come and go. They turn sour, become destructive, even harmful, if we try to embalm them. In those moments when Grace abounds, we have to flow with them. The Spirit of God comes and goes like the wind—as Jesus said—but when we try to close the window to capture it, the wind ceases to move at all.

Past moments are for remembering. Future moments are the source of hope. But life must be lived in the present moment. Now is the time to live, neither shackled by the past nor escaping into the future. Life does not last forever. We must learn to enjoy the moments of Grace which are given to us. We need to receive them with open hands, trusting their goodness and enjoying them for the time. We come to value their preciousness precisely because they will pass.

The old world, however, always beckons us back. Its appeal is the predictability, and certainty, of pat answers. Its danger is that it seeks to lock God in a cage where he can be tamed and made sensible and safe. The old world emasculates in the name of safety. A childhood story of Sam Keen comes to mind. A mighty horse was kept in a vacant lot near his home in the city:

> A stallion lived there in an enclosure hardly large enough for a backyard barbecue. Most afternoons after school I went to visit him. He must have been seventeen-hands high—chestnut colored with a wide blaze in the middle of his nose. His muscles danced wildly inside a shining coat. He was, altogether, a horse fit for a minor divinity to ride into battle. Once when his owner allowed a friend to take him out of the corral I got to ride him in a large field down by the river. It was like all the outlaws in all the movies riding toward freedom. That is, until he sniffed a mare in some unknown pasture and took off like hell. The owner finally had to rescue both of us, and he returned my friend to prison and was none too happy with me for not being able to control the stallion. Not long after the owner decided the horse would have to be gelded. He wasn't safe to keep in suburbia. And he asked me if I would come on the following Saturday to help the veterinarian with the job.

Do you leave your god to suffer alone
Or share his pain?

For some reason that took half a lifetime to understand, I went. The veterinarian arrived, gave the necessary shots to deaden the consciousness and the pain. The stallion was eased off his feet and rested on the ground. The incisions were made. The testicles with their long roots reaching up into the fire in the stomach were removed. The wound cauterized. And the stunned horse struggled to his feet.

I vomited.

I suppose he was gentle afterwards and could be ridden. I never went to visit him again.

I wish I had not shared in the violation of that Saturday morning. It seems better to fail a hundred times, to be thrown time and again to the ground than to tame the wild god.[21]

The old world, in a thousand ways, seeks to tame the wild God, the God of Grace. But he keeps breaking into life—our life—in amazing ways. The Good News is that he cannot be tamed. He makes life new because he is forever restless and insists on creating us in his image. He is on the move and calls us to come follow. The Divine restlessness is mirrored in our restlessness. The Bible boldly assumes that our restlessness is God's calling to come dance with him in that crazy world known as the kingdom of God.

Crazy Life

To characterize life in the Kingdom as crazy is certainly not the traditional way of describing it, but it does have the advantage of being true to the experience of many of us. In the motion picture *The Stunt Man,* Peter O'Toole plays the part of a movie director who not only directs the film on which he is working, but also the lives of all those with whom he comes in contact. One of the characters says of him, "He's not evil; just a little crazy. He's a crazy man." Some of us experience the second half of life in a similar way and are led to suspect that God is not evil, just a little crazy. He is a crazy God, and it is a crazy life. Consider, for example, Abraham's experience:

Now the LORD said to Abram, "Go from your country and your kindred and your father's house to the land that I will show you.

And I will make of you a great nation, and I will bless you, and make your name great . . . ."

So Abram went, as the LORD had told him . . . . Abram was seventy-five years old when he departed from Haran. And Abram took Sarai his wife, and Lot his brother's son, and all their possessions . . . and they set forth to go to the land of Canaan. (Gen. 12:1-5)

Why would God's calling come to a man seventy-five years old? Abram was over the hill. He had done it all. At seventy-five you look back with satisfaction or regret, but in any case you expect God to come to you with a word of comfort, not some adventurous idea. In his late seventies, my father was ill and in the hospital. As a loyal and loving son, I tried to cheer him with interesting chatter. But he looked at me and said, "Son, you sound like a well man talking to a sick man." At seventy-five, who needs a calling? At seventy-five, you want to hear a word of commendation, "Well done, good and faithful servant."

But, no, this Bible story implies that relationship with God is full of surprises. When we come to the Bible, we find a strange world about a crazy God. Karl Barth describes our feelings:

Once more we stand before this "other" new world which begins in the Bible. In it the chief consideration is not the doings of man but the doings of God . . . not industry, honesty, and helpfulness as we may practice them in our old ordinary world, but the establishment and growth of a new world, . . . in which God and *his* morality reign. In the light of this coming world a David is a great man in spite of his adultery and bloody sword . . . [and] Into this world the publicans and the harlots will go before your impeccably elegant and righteous folk of good society! In this world the true hero is the lost son, who is absolutely lost and feeding swine—and not his moral elder brother! . . . We may . . . say: I do not need this; I do not desire it; it tells me nothing; I cannot get anywhere with it! [It is as if, however, the Word says, at every step,] "What interest have I in your 'practical life'? I have little to do with that. Follow after *me* or let me go my way!"[22]

At seventy-five, all of us would agree, Abram had earned his right to ease. He had earned the right to say, "Let somebody else do it. The younger generation has vim, vigor, and vitality. But I'm tired; I am seventy-five years old. You can't teach an old dog new tricks." And then the word of God comes, as if deaf to Abraham's concerns, and says, "Now, let's get started." The author calls attention to his age because, in this crazy life, living with a crazy God, we are to understand that nothing is ever settled, nothing is ever nailed down, and when we least expect it, the Spirit blows in our ear and whispers, "You're wanted on the phone."

Nor does an examination of the message to Abram do anything to change our perception that we are dealing with a crazy God. The word that comes to Abram asks him to leave his relatives and all of those who matter most to him. He has to leave his business and the turf that has become so familiar to him. "Abram," God says, "I want you to pull up your roots, take on a different identity and begin a new life." Notice the story does not lead us to think that all of the experiences which have made up his life to this point contributed to this peak experience, as though the calling were the culmination of all that had gone before. It is not as though God is saying, "All of your life has prepared you for this moment, Abram." Rather, the word comes and says, "Everything up to this point is irrelevant. Now you can begin to live. You're seventy-five and we have to hurry. This new life, this new identity is so radical a change that it will require a new name. Abram doesn't fit what I have in mind. How does Abraham strike you?"

Some of us know something about that kind of dislocation. Many have experienced the kind of disruption which comes in the middle of life. But others are yet unprepared. Carl Jung, the psychiatrist, laments,

> The worst of it all is that intelligent and cultivated people live their lives without even knowing of the possibility of such transformations. Wholly unprepared, they embark upon the second half of life. Or are there perhaps colleges for forty-year-olds which prepare them for their coming life and its demands as the ordinary colleges introduce our young people to a knowledge of the world? No, thoroughly unprepared we take the step into the afternoon of life; worse still, we take this step with the false assumption that our truths and ideals will serve us as hitherto. But we cannot live the afternoon of life according to the programme of life's morning; for what was great in the morning will be of little value at evening, and what in the morning was true will at evening have bedcome a lie.[23]

Jung's clinical experience and this archetypical story of encounter with God remind us that the old ties, the old arrangements, the old definitions that served so well, can get in the way of God's calling, and must be discarded. Jesus says cryptically, "Do not think that I have come to bring peace on earth; I have not come to bring peace, but a sword" (Matt. 10:34). A sword is for cutting and severing. He adds definition to the severing process. "For I have come to set a man against his father, and a daughter against her mother, and a daughter-in-law against her mother-in-law; and a man's foes will be those of his own household" (Matt. 10:35-36). He invites us to take the journey into the Kingdom but warns that we cannot return to bury our relatives. (Cf. Matt. 8:22.) Nostalgia for the old life has no place in the new land. "No one who puts his hand to the plow and looks back is fit for the kingdom of God" (Luke 9:62). One of the most disturbing things about this crazy God and the crazy life he invites us to live is that it upsets the traditional cultural and religious values to which we have grown accustomed.

Hosea's experience highlights the scandalous disregard of God for traditional values. The prophet was a promising young theologian, on his way up; a bright future ahead of him. "The man most likely to succeed," his colleagues might have said. Probably would have been voted "Seminarian of the Year," had there been such awards. But he got off the track somehow. He married a prostitute. Not the kind of minister's wife a parish is apt to embrace. Crazy man! He babbled on about his experience with her although she kept running off with other men, and each time he would take her back. No pride I suppose. And then children came along. Hosea gave them terrible names. The first child he called "Hiroshima," (a rough translation) as a kind of reminder of all the sinfulness in the world. His wife bore him another child by one of her lovers, and this one Hosea named "Not to be pitied." His friends no doubt shook their heads in despair and thought he was clearly out of his mind, especially when he claimed *God* told him what to name the children. A third child he named, simply, "Not my child." Imagine the poor children having to bear those names for a lifetime!

Obviously, Hosea marched to a different drummer. He was tuned to a different wavelength than everyone else. Hosea could no more explain his actions to his colleagues than a butterfly emerging from a cocoon can communicate with its former caterpillar comrades. Were it not for the fact that Hosea's story, like Abraham's, is in the Bible, we would call them both insane. Because they enjoy biblical sanction, the offensiveness of their behavior is overlooked and the point missed by those of us who want to settle down to be secure and comfortable.

This brings us to perhaps the most bizarre aspect of Abraham's story. He had the audacity to call his actions "God's will." No doubt the citizens of Ur talked about Abraham after he left home, pulling up roots and leaving the business in the way he did. But for them the sure sign of his insanity was the way he went off muttering, "This is God's calling."

We think we understand God and therefore assume his ways are predictable. We forget that God's foolishness is our wisdom, and our wisdom and sanity is to God crazy stupidity. The divine calling to Abraham made as much sense as though the president of the United States were to resign and join the Communist Party, calling it "God's will"; or as though the chairman of the board of General Motors were to leave the company so he could become one of Nader's raiders, saying, "I have seen the light." It is like our sixty-year-old Dutch doctor friend, who, after 264 days of sailing alone around the world, came back home and said that he had undertaken the thirty-thousand-mile voyage to realize a boyhood dream. Crazy old man!

What is there in Abraham's experience that would lead him to speak of such craziness as "God's calling?" Are we dealing here with some kind of rationalization? Is it no more than a justification of deviant behavior? Is Abraham an early edition of Flip Wilson? "God made me do it." How does Abraham's experience differ from that of going into a travel agency, seeing a number of alluring brochures, and signing up for a cruise or going on vacation for a change of scenery? How does his change of vocational location differ from reading the want ads in the newspaper and responding to an out-of-town job offer? We can understand Abraham's move as an advancement to better himself, but what does it mean to speak of it as "God's calling?" Indeed, amidst all the voices in our culture that call us to buy their product, align ourselves with this group, or to enlist in that cause, how are we to know which, if any, are the call of God?

Keen's experience is again helpful. In speaking autobiographically of his own journey, he says:

When I reached the point where the traditional covenants— church, university—were killing me, I had to make the choice between discontinuity and death. I knew at the time I broke continuity that there was something terribly tragic about it. I knew my decision involved cruelties and hurting people. But, somehow, I knew that in order to live I had to make those decisions.[24]

Keen's experience reminds us that in every moment of life we face choices between life and death. Our decisions are pregnant with significance because they determine whether we live and grow, or wither and die. Our openness to the possibilities of life indicates our willingness to respond to God's calling. God is the Lord of life and growth. He calls us into life and energizes our growth. Because all living things are growing things, life and growth become synonymous. They are God's will.

Meister Eckhart was once asked what God did all day with his time. "Why, God births," was the reply. God delights in birthing. Life and growth become the criteria for hearing and understanding what, in each moment of experience, is the calling of God. Our whole being is focused on living. We might call it the instinct to survive, or the will to live, but there is in all of us that instinctive response to our Creator. It is the instinct to respond to the dance of life.

Now, to be sure, there are many ways to grow and many opportunities or possibilities in any given moment of experience. The person, for example, whose experience contains the verdict, "You are terminally ill with cancer," can either respond by saying, "I am to die of cancer" or "I am to live with cancer." Both are possible in that moment, but clearly one perspective opens options that the other does not. The same can be said for growing older. It is happening to all of us, day by day, bit by bit, inch by inch. The years add up and fly by us ever more swiftly. We can see aging as a decline and wait for the approach of death, or as a call to different service, using different gifts. Tennyson saw the possibilities:

> ... you and I are old:
> Old age hath yet his honor and his toil;
> Death closes all; but something ere the end,
> Some work of noble note, may yet be done,
> Not unbecoming men that strove with Gods.[25]

I have a cousin who lived in Princeton, New Jersey, well into her nineties. If there was a cause in which she could enlist,

Cousin Edith was found carrying a placard on the street, demonstrating with the youngest. Her home was an open house to world travelers. She lived every moment, responding to the calling of God to live and grow.

The more we are able to say, "Yes" to life; the more we are able to embrace it, unconditionally, the more we are able, by faith, to speak of God's calling.

One way, therefore, of knowing God's calling is to examine each moment of our lives and identify those components that lead to life and growth—risky though they may seem. Birthing is always characterized by a sense of risk and adventure. Boredom and death are characterized by security and routine. Abraham may have been bored. Or the grasslands may have withered, necessitating his moving on. Perhaps he was no longer challenged. Maybe he had dreamed all his dreams. Whatever it was, the restlessness opened him to the new possibilities inherent in the experience. In the risk of grasping them, Abraham was accounted a man of faith who responded to "the call of God."

In our experience, God's calling is not obviously nor necessarily "religious." Religion has no exclusive claim upon life and growth. Abraham may well have dropped by a travel agency and been enamored by the four-color brochure luring him to Canaan, but it was in the creative possibilities for his life that Abraham felt the lure to pull up roots and move on.

It is this pulling up of roots and moving on that so often characterizes God's calling at mid-life. Quoting, again, Keen's experience: a modern version of Abraham's story:

As I understand the second part of life, my task is to destroy what I built in the first part of my life. At about the age of forty, I began to be very tired of being Sam Keen. All the character armor I had built up in the first part of my life—the modes of coping, the intellectual way of unifying and ordering the world, my defense system—began to crumble. The second part of my life appears radically discontinuous with the first part of my life. I no longer know where I am going. I do not have organized futures. I cannot control things. Now I experience life as much more benevolent. The less I control and the less I order, the more certain I am that there is already an ordering principle built into the universe.[26]

In their respective journeys, both men found life to be a dance with the crazy God. I take it that the art of graceful dancing is in trusting our partner. God invites us to dance every moment with him, but there is a certain hesitancy on our part. We are afraid to step forth because we do not know the name of the tune. We are sure we will be clumsy and fall on our faces. We fear making mistakes or embarrassing ourselves. So we hang back like wallflowers. We want to sit this one out. We choose to live with the familiar certainties. To the degree that we close ourselves off from the call to live and to grow, to that degree we close ourselves off from the crazy God who invites us to come dance with him.

Clearly, the identification of God's calling is not an exact science. There is risk involved. We risk being mistaken in identifying what is, for us, life or what our growth requires. There is always the danger of rationalization, but, even behind the rationalization, there is yet the reality of the pressure or urge, working through our restlessness, which must be trusted. Howard Thurman once observed that behind our purposes there is a Purpose. Behind our wisdom there is a Wisdom. We might add that behind our rationalization there is a Truth seeking expression. God's call, therefore, is to be found in every drop of experience. It is a call characterized by that restlessness that pressures us to lean into life and grasp its possibilities while we yet breathe.

Mid-life restlessness makes us aware that there is a certain urgency about the business of living. We do not have all the time in the world to be about it. Our restlessness must be given heed and the risks taken. When it dawns on us that we are all terminal cases, we can begin to make some life choices.

The invitation that comes to us in mid-life urges us to embrace life and say yes to those inner nudgings of the Spirit that begin to emerge within us and haunt us. It is the invitation to trust what Keen calls the benevolent "ordering principle of the universe" or what the story of Abraham gives us permission to call "God."

Falling Upward

To risk embarking on the crazy mid-life journey, clearly, requires permission in advance to make mistakes. We are sailing uncharted waters and exploring new frontiers in our lives. Saying yes to life is dangerous because in responding to God's call to live there are no guarantees. We may make false starts, take wrong turns, end up in blind alleys. Restlessness, response, and risk all go together. The paradigm story of this trinitarian aspect of life is the biblical tale of Adam and Eve and their temptation.

And the Lord God planted a garden in Eden, in the east; and there he put the man whom he had formed . . . . And the LORD God commanded the man, saying, "You may freely eat of every tree of the garden; but of the tree of the knowledge of good and evil you shall not eat, for in the day that you eat of it you shall die . . . ."

Now the serpent was more subtle than any other wild creature that the Lord God had made. He said to the woman, "Did God say, 'You shall not eat of any tree of the garden'?" And the woman said to the serpent, "We may eat of the fruit of the trees of the garden; but God said, 'You shall not eat of the fruit of the tree which is in the midst of the garden, neither shall you touch it, lest you die.'" But the serpent said to the woman, "You will not die. For God knows that when you eat of it your eyes will be opened, and you will be like God, knowing good and evil." So when the woman saw that the tree was good for food, and that it was a delight to the eyes, and that the tree was to be desired to make one wise, she took of its fruit and ate; and she also gave some to her husband, and he ate. Then the eyes of both were opened, and they knew that they were naked; and they sewed fig leaves together and made themselves aprons. (Gen. 2:8—3:7)

Since the task of Christian theology is to interpret life from the perspective of the Resurrection, we need to put on the spectacles of faith in order to look at this pre-Christian account of the "fall" of the human race. The task is to understand this story of disobedience and corruption as Good News, transformed by Resurrection faith.

Let us dismiss at the outset any literal interpretation of the Garden of Eden story. This means not only dismissing it as a scientific account of how the world was created in six days and the human race drawn from a man and a woman named Adam and Eve but also as a history of a time *before* the Fall.

It is interesting that enlightened Christians who can see the difficulty in a literal understanding of creation in six days and of the race descending from one man and one woman, nevertheless fall into the trap of believing that the state of being before the Fall can be spoken of historically. This belief holds that return to such a state is desirable and worthy of our prayers. Return to those idyllic, romantic, childlike days in the Garden before the Fall would solve all the problems of the world.

But what would such life be like? At best we would have to say that life in the Garden of Eden would be a life of childlike innocence: preadult, with neither maturity born of experience nor character born of testing. At worst, life before the Fall would have meant bondage to what we might call "The Eden Ethos": a life of enslavement, blindly and unthinkingly following rules of behavior like obedient sheep.

The feminist movement has some grasp of this kind of enslavement and offers us an analogy. It has made us aware of our obedience to cultural mores, which are all the more insidious precisely because they have never been legislated and, therefore, have never been submitted to examination, discussion, or vote. Regulation by roles and rules that are part of a cultural ethos is all the more binding in its enslavement.

Rosemary Daniell describes the plight of southern womenhood in her book *Fatal Flowers: On Sin, Sex and Suicide in the Deep South*. She chafes under the bondage of a cultural ethos; unquestioned rules by which we have lived.

> I perceived my mother, grandmothers, sister, daughters—and all the women whose roots I shared—as netted in one mutual silken bondage. Together, we were trapped in a morass of Spanish moss, Bible Belt guilt, and the pressures of a patriarchy stronger than in any other part of the country.[27]

Neither the childlike innocence of Eden before the Fall, nor the enslavement to its ethos does justice to the size and integrity of human dignity.

If, then, we are not to take the Genesis story of creation literally (that is, historically), how are we to understand it? As it stands, the story clearly offers a theological perspective on life. It is an interpretation of the human experience; and, more specifically, it is an interpretation of the moral experience of knowing the difference between right and wrong, good and evil. The bottom line, so far as the story is concerned, is simply that it is better *not* to know the difference. Knowledge of right and wrong, good and evil, is bad for us.

But such an assertion must be challenged. I, for one, do not believe that it is better to live in childlike innocence, nor do I believe it is better to live in bondage to rules and roles that have never been questioned. If my forty some odd years have done nothing else, they have convinced me that the knowledge of good and evil is not morally inferior to innocence and enslavement. Paul Tillich puts it memorably:

A morality which plays safe, by subjecting itself to an unconditional authority, is suspect. It has not the courage to take guilt and tragedy upon itself. True morality is a morality of risk. It is a morality which is based on the "courage to be," the dynamic self-affirmation of man as man.[28]

Left then, as it is, this pre-Christian story of the Fall of the human race, this story of corruption and disobedience, hardly qualifies as Good News.

So, back to the drawing board. As was said earlier, the task of Christian theology is always to interpret life from the perspective of the Resurrection. It is an unnerving characteristic of the Resurrection to invert things. For example, the Resurrection turns death into life and endings into beginnings. The function, therefore, of Resurrection theology is to look at this story and invert it in such a way that we can see it as Good News for the mid-life journey.

Fortunately, we do not have to start from scratch. There were some Christian thinkers known as Gnostics who lived in the early days of the church. They looked at this story through the eyes of Resurrection faith and saw its inversion. The Gnostic account of the Genesis story goes something like this:

Once upon a time the Divine Father created the world and everything in it, including Adam and Eve, the first people. Then, as is so often the case with the male ego, the Divine Father began to think more highly of himself than was warranted and laid upon the human race certain prescriptions and laws, obedience to which was designed to satisfy his Divine Ego. Fortunately, the Divine Mother, Sophia, the source of wisdom, saw the plight of Adam and Eve. So she sent a serpent as her messenger to inform them about the true nature of their situation: they were free to live and to enjoy life. The serpent conveyed the message. Enlightened by this knowledge, Adam and Eve challenged the rules, ate the forbidden fruit, and discovered they were, in fact, free. Their eyes were opened, and they knew the difference between good and evil.

Now that may seem like a rather bizarre reading of the Genesis story, but it has one interesting characteristic which is, for our purposes, significant: inversion, the changing of death to life. The Fall, in this Gnostic understanding of the creation story, is seen as a Fall *upward*. Prior to the Fall, there was no difference between Adam and Eve and the guppies that swam in the primordial pools, or the trees that produced seeds each according to its own kind, mutely obeying the genetic law inscribed within them. The distinguishing characteristic of Adam and Eve after the Fall is their knowledge of good and evil. After the Fall upward, human beings knew they had a choice, something that fish do not know, nor have. Nor do trees and mountains, nor the heavens above, however vast they may be.

The dignity of being human does not depend upon our innocence but on how much life we can embrace, how much understanding of the great adventure we can encompass. Keen, reflecting on his experience, puts it this way:

> I believe the most potent action comes from those persons who have been scarred and healed a thousand times. We act not as innocent children of the cosmos but as historical persons who have become gnarled and seasoned.[29]

Clearly the decision of Adam and Eve is not some trivial act. To eat the forbidden fruit is to rebel against the divine admonition to stay innocent and immature. Their rebellion is an act of total will. It is an act, if you will, of total self-affirmation. Thurman characterizes such an act of self-affirmation:

> It is not a unilateral act in the midst of other unilateral acts on the part of the individual. It is, rather, an ingathering of all the phases of one's being, a creative summary of the individual's life—it is a saturation of the self with the mood and the integrity of assent. Something total within the man says "Yes."[30]

To say yes is to offer oneself totally to Life, for "Life" is simply another name for the God of Grace.

Adam and Eve challenged the arbitrary and external god of Authority in response to the inner urging of the Ground of their Being, the God within. The moral imperative of life is not some strange alien law that is imposed upon our being but rather the Law of Being itself. The point of the story is that we cannot be obedient to the commands of a stranger, even if he is a god. Morality is self-affirmation; it is embracing the gift of life with the totality of our being. It is the only response pleasing to the Living God.

One of the almost forgotten stories that came out of the Iranian hostage crisis is illustrative. When the American captives were finally released from captivity, their families breathed a sigh of relief and the nation rejoiced. The negotiations for their release had been successful. The returning hostages were seen as heroic patriots. But the earlier reaction to the pilgrimage of Barbara Thiem, forty-one-year-old mother of one of the hostages, was more ambivalent. She defied the State Department, the authority of the President, and the will of this country in order to go to Iran to see her son. Time reported some of the reaction to her visit:

> Some townspeople consider her a traitor for going off to Iran against the Administration's wishes . . . [others thought of her as a heroine]. Her younger sister, Judy [said]: "She's not a traitor, and she's not Joan of Arc. She's just a mother who wants to see her son."[31]

Barbara Thiem had to say yes to the God of her Being even though it meant defying the gods of civil authority and public opinion. She had to see her son. She exemplifies what Adam and Eve discovered: Before we achieve our selfhood, or attain autonomous maturity, we must disown all of those "virtues" and "vices" laid upon us by external authorities, human or divine. We must take upon ourselves the responsibility for our lives. To be created in the image of God is to accept responsibility for being the creator of our own values. In Adam and Eve's passion for life, in their challenge of those arbitrary rules, they assumed the guilt of rebellion but discovered the dignity of being human. Adam and Eve took the fruit and ate it. They said yes to life. Their eyes were opened, and they knew the difference between good and evil. The rest of their days were spent in making choices.

On Being Perfect

Unfortunately, the theology of permission, i.e., to choose and thus risk making mistakes, seems to founder on the brutal rock of Jesus' words, "You, therefore, must be perfect, as your heavenly Father is perfect" (Matt. 5:48). If we are required to be perfect, we (like the rich young man in the Bible who couldn't part with his wealth, Matt. 19:16-22) must leave in a state of despair. We know that we cannot be so. If nothing else, middle age has taught us that much! Perfection, as we use the term, means measurement by, or comparison to, an external norm. We speak of machining an airplane part to within one ten-thousandth of an inch of perfection. And since the moral norm about which Jesus is speaking requires that we be measured against God's perfection, we find ourselves in a no-win situation. God may be perfect, but we know that we are not, nor can we be. The outlook is bleak. If we believe we must be perfect as God is perfect, we are condemned to a life of futility and guilt.

It is no accident that the saints of the church spent so much time in prayer and confession. The more we approach moral perfection, the more do we become aware of the flaws that separate us from our goal. As in driving toward the Grand Canyon, the closer we come to it the larger does the chasm loom before us. The Apostle Paul, who tried the road of moral perfection before us, uttered the universal complaint, "The good that I would do, I do not do; and that which I know I should not do, is what I end up doing. Oh wretched man that I am, who can deliver me from such bondage?" (paraphrase of Rom. 7:19, 24).

But what if the perfection Jesus was talking about is not a measurement or a comparison to an external norm? What if it is something entirely different?

Instinctively, we have used the term perfection in quite another way. We speak, for example of a "perfect sunset" when we see the sky set aglow in the evening. Clearly we do not mean such a sunset is measured by, or compared with, other sunsets. Each one is different. There are no two alike. There can be no external norm for comparison. The perfection of the sunset is not dependent upon past or future sunsets for its worth or valuing as a "perfect one." Similarly, when Jesus says God is perfect, he is not talking about comparing his Father with other gods. God's perfection is to be found only within himself. He is to be compared with no one. Isaiah makes the point with fine sarcasm,

> Who has measured the waters in the hollow of his hand
> and marked off the heavens with a span . . . ?

Who has directed the Spirit of the Lord,
  or as his counselor has instructed him?
Whom did he consult for his enlightenment,
  and who taught him the path of justice,
and taught him knowledge,
  and showed him the way of understanding?

The questions are rhetorical. The answer is assumed by Isaiah: No one.

To whom then will you liken God,
  or what likeness compare with him? . . .
Have you not known? Have you not heard?
  Has it not been told you from the beginning?
  Have you not understood from the foundations of the earth?
It is he who sits above the circle of the earth,
  and its inhabitants are like grasshoppers;
who stretches out the heavens like a curtain,
  and spreads them like a tent to dwell in;
who brings princes to nought,
  and makes the rulers of the earth as nothing.
Scarcely are they planted, scarcely sown,
  scarcely has their stem taken root in the earth,
when he blows upon them, and they wither,
  and the tempest carries them off like stubble.
To whom then will you compare me,
  that I should be like him? says the Holy One. (Isa. 40:12-25)

By the time Isaiah has finished, it is clear that God is One of a kind. There is nothing to which God's perfection can be compared.

Similarly, when Jesus tells us we are to be perfect as God is perfect, he is not saying that we are to be compared with some external norm of perfection outside of ourselves. Each of us is different. There are no two of us alike. We are unique. We cannot be compared to other human beings. Rather, we are to be compared only to our one-of-a-kindness. It is absurd to say that a redhead is a more perfect human being than a blond. Or that a person six feet tall is a more perfect human being than one five feet four inches tall. William Robert McClelland is a one-of-a-kind human being. When Jesus says to me I am to be perfect as God is perfect, it can only mean that I am to be perfect as William Robert McClelland, and not as John Doe or Mary Doaks, much less God. My perfection is to be measured by the potential of *my* being. I am to be who *I* am. Jesus is calling me to be me, and no one else.

In the legend of King Arthur and the knights of the Round Table, a vision of the holy grail comes to Sir Gawain. He vows to set off in search of it the very next day. All the other knights of the Round Table vow that they, too, will go in search of the sacred chalice. But they will not journey together. As dawn breaks the following morning, each of the knights enters the forest—alone—where he perceives it to be the darkest and the thickest. None of the knights follow a pathway. To follow a pathway is to go where someone else has already searched.

Perfection, like the search for the holy grail, is not something we find by walking someone else's path. Perfection is not a norm external to our being and to which we are compared. It is rather the internal possibility of our becoming. To be perfect as God is perfect is to come to know who we are and must be.

There is a sense of guilt which accompanies the failure to be perfect. But it is not from failing to measure up to someone else's standard. That is sick guilt, and it immobilizes us. It is what McLeish calls "the sick scent of dung under our fingernails." Real guilt comes from our failure to discover the miracle of our own unique life. I cannot imagine anything more horrible than coming to the end of life with the realization that William Robert McClelland had not lived it to its fullest, that he had not drunk the cup of each moment to the bottom. The cup that life hands me to drink is, of course, different from the cup which it hands you. That is another reason why understanding perfection as comparison—one life with another—is futile. I cannot drink your cup of life, but I can drink mine. Indeed, no one can do it for me. True guilt, healthy guilt, motivates us rather than incapacitates us. It comes, not from comparing cups, but from the realization that we have failed to drink the cup that is ours.

Jesus tried to dislodge from the minds of his followers the concept of perfection that produces unhealthy guilt. He did so by referring to the Law: the external norm of moral perfection.

"If you would enter life," [Jesus said,] "keep the commandments." [A young man] said to him, "Which?" And jesus said, "You shall not kill, You shall not commit adultery, You shall not steal, You shall not bear false witness, Honor your father and mother, and, You shall love your neighbor as yourself." The young man said to him, "All these I have observed; what do I still lack?" Jesus said to him, "If you would be perfect, go, sell what you possess and give to the poor, and you will have treasure in heaven; and come, follow me." When the young man heard this he went away sorrowful; for he had great possessions. (Matt. 19:17-22)

The young man in the story asks, "What must I do to have eternal life?" It is a bad question because he is assuming that salvation is to *do* something rather than to *be* someone. As his response to Jesus indicates, he believes salvation is found by fulfilling perfectly the obligations of God's Law. He is, therefore, on a different wavelength than Jesus. But Jesus answers his bad question with an obviously absurd answer designed to display the impossibility of ever being saved, given the young man's premise. Jesus says, in effect, "If you want to be perfect, keep all of the commandments."

We must remember that Jesus has earlier redefined all the commandments in such a way that it is obvious no one can keep them. (See Matt. 5:21-30.) To commit adultery is not to go to bed with someone else's spouse but rather to think about it. To kill is not simply to commit an act of murder but to be angry with the other person. Nevertheless, the young man claims that he has kept all of the commandments. He thinks he is well on his way to perfection. So Jesus, with a twinkle in his eyes, decides to teach him a lesson and says, "If you really want to be perfect, then go and sell all that you have and come, follow me."

The young man went away sorrowful. He discovered what age teaches: none of us is perfect. Both the advantage and disadvantage of youth is that it is given to fantasy. This young man's fantasy was that he thought he had kept all of the law. In reality, he found he could not part with his money and was thus disillusioned. We all fall short at some point. That is what Jesus wanted him—and us—to discover.

Unfortunately, most of us have been brought up to think that Jesus was always serious and, therefore, have missed his sense of humor as well as the point of this story. We have assumed Jesus meant for us to measure up to an external norm such as a set of commandments, when, in reality, he was trying to demonstrate the impossibility of perfect obedience. Measuring ourselves against the specification of someone else's blueprint is frustrating at best and deadly at worst. Trying to fulfill external expectations can take a tragic toll, as this poignant poem "About School" illustrates:

He always wanted to say things. But no one understood.
He always wanted to explain things. But no one cared.
So he drew.

Sometimes he would just draw and it wasn't anything. He wanted
to carve it in stone or write it in the sky.
He would lie out on the grass and look up in the sky and it would
be only him and the sky and the things inside that needed saying.

And it was after that, that he drew the picture. It was a beautiful
picture. He kept it under the pillow and would let no one see it.
And he would look at it every night and think about it. And
when it was dark, and his eyes were closed, he could still see it.
And it was all of him. And he loved it.

When he started school he brought it with him. Not to show
anyone, but just to have with him like a friend.

It was funny about school.
He sat in a square, brown desk like all the other square, brown
desks and he thought it should be red.
And his room was a square, brown room. Like all the other
rooms. And it was tight and close. And stiff.

He hated to hold the pencil and the chalk, with his arm stiff and
his feet flat on the floor, stiff, with the teacher watching and
watching.
And then he had to write numbers. And they weren't anything.
They were worse than the letters that could be something if you
put them together.
And the numbers were tight and square and he hated the whole
thing.

The teacher came and spoke to him. She told him to wear a tie
like all the other boys. He said he didn't like them and she said it
didn't matter.
After that they drew. And he drew all yellow and it was the way
he felt about morning. And it was beautiful.

The teacher came and smiled at him, "What's this?" she said.
"Why don't you draw something like Ken's drawing? Isn't that
beautiful?
It was all questions.

After that his mother bought him a tie and he always drew
airplanes and rocket ships like everyone else. And he threw the
old picture away.

59

And when he lay out alone looking at the sky, it was big and blue and all of everything, but he wasn't anymore.

He was square inside and brown, and his hands were stiff, and he was like anyone else. And the thing inside him that needed saying didn't need saying anymore.

It had stopped pushing. It was crushed. Stiff
Like everything else.[32]

This poem was turned in to a teacher in Regina, Saskatchewan, by a senior in high school. He committed suicide a few weeks later.

In one way or another, trying to measure up to someone else's standard is a dead end. Just as God insists on being perfect, that is, being who he is, so Jesus is saying we must insist on being who we are. Being perfect as our Heavenly Father is perfect means risking living the one life that has been given us. It means becoming the miracle, the once-in-a-universe possibility that is you and me.

Chapter Three

Second Childhood
and the Juvenile Delinquent

The Child Within

To speak of middle age as a miracle time in which we can realize our unique potential is not how we generally regard that period of our life. Instead the mid-life journey is often referred to as a "second childhood." There are, indeed, similarities between a first and a second childhood; and the reference could be commendable were it not for the fact that we generally hold the first childhood in such low regard. For example, not too long ago I caught myself asking a youngster, "What do you want to do when you grow up?" Fortunately, I caught myself and did not insult the child by getting the question entirely out of my mouth. The question is asked often enough of children by well-meaning adults, but it lacks imagination.

In the first place the question depreciates the *now* of childhood. It assumes that the really important time is in the future when the child has grown up. The "grown up" time matters, but *now* does not. Being a child is just a stage to grow through until *that* time later on when it really counts.

The question is also based upon an erroneous assumption of a time in our lives when we can say, "We have grown up." We accept the fact that children grow and develop, but we assume adults "have arrived." Adults have their act together. They have grown up. We speak of maturity as if it were a static state of being. As a result, those times of stress and strain that unsettle us as adults and leave us feeling uncertain are viewed with embarrassment at best, and suspicion at worst. The mid-life journey is regarded as a regression: a return to childhood—a second childhood.

The fact of the matter is, of course, that throughout our lives we continue to grow and mature. Growing is a continuous and never-ending process with our bodies generating new cells to replace the ones that wear out and our minds assessing a lifetime of experiences in a function known as learning. Only death pulls the plug. Usually we are unaware of the growth changes taking place in our body, but the maturing process occurring in our psyche is felt within us as a crisis of identity. We leave behind a familiar but too restrictive view of life as we enlarge our vision.

We can be grateful, therefore, to those growing adults who have left behind some record of their pilgrimage—footprints that the rest of us can follow in deriving some understanding of what is happening to us. Sam Keen was for me such a trailblazer and I have spoken of him often. In his very helpful book *Beginnings Without End,* he warns that,

The major discipline [of the adult years] is negotiating those turbulent passages that seem to come every ten years or so. The task of making the young into prematurely peaceful beings is comical. Wisdom is a vice at twenty and a necessity at sixty. There is a time for adolescent insanity and the folly of second childhood, and a time for planning, renunciation and work. Most of what we call happiness is only a matter of knowing what time it is and not taking clues from anyone else's clock.[33]

Gail Sheehy also offers helpful observations about those crisis, growth periods.

The work of adult life is not easy. As in childhood, each step presents not only new tasks of development but requires a letting go of the techniques that worked before. With each passage some magic must be given up, some cherished illusion of safety and comfortably familiar sense of self must be cast off, to allow for the greater expansion of our own distinctiveness . . . . [Maturity is overcoming] the false expectation that the roles and rules, the dreams and ideals that may have served well in the first half of life will carry over into the second. They do not; they cannot. The second half of life must have its own significance.[34]

Carl Jung, one of the major architects of modern psychiatry, also regards the second half of life as having a unique significance. He claims that as human beings we spend the first half of our lives taking our identity cues from the outside world. We let others define us and our roles in life. The first half of our lives are spent responding rationally to the cues given by society in order to measure up to its expectations and take our place responsibly in its ranks. But, writes Jung, the major task of the last half of life is to get in touch with the inner self and especially that spontaneous, uninhibited little child who was left behind and ignored in the rush to live in the world of adult expectations and definitions, a world governed by responsible, rational, common sense. The mid-life journey offers a chance to get acquainted with the child within.

Sitting in the airport one day, I noticed a family of two little children and a mother. The mother was reading a paperback, trying to concentrate on her reading while waiting to board the plane, but the children had other things to do. They were exploring the carry-on luggage of all the passengers who were sitting in the waiting area. When they tired of that, the contents of the ashtrays seemed to fascinate them. In exasperation the mother pulled the children over to her and made them sit by her side. Before she could find her place in the story and continue reading, however, the children were exploring her pocketbook.

There is something about children that is instinctively inquisitive; a trait that cannot be denied nor ignored. Given half a chance, it will come out in some exuberant, exciting adventurous way. It is in light of this natural behavior of children—the urge to grasp all of life's wonderful opportunities, an urge which will not be repressed—that Jesus' words must be understood: "Let the children come to me, do not hinder them; for to such belongs the kingdom of God" (Mark 10:14). Unless we become like that little child inside us, we will never know the Kingdom.

In most cases it is tragically true that the little child in us has been buried. As adults we have sold our souls to the company store. We have permitted others to lay on us the rules of the game and the roles by which we live. It may be the company, it may be a spouse. It may be friends, or it may be parents. It could be the church. During our early years we operate dutifully out of a sense of what we *should* do. We want to please and be accepted. But then in our thirties we begin to get in touch with another part of ourselves. A certain restlessness begins to emerge and we know we *want* to do certain things with our lives. The restlessness grows until in our forties and fifties it has become a resounding "You *must* do them *now*. We sense that time is running out on us. We realize we do not have all the time in the world to discover the purpose and miracle of our own unique being.

Hannah Tillich's poignant observation of her husband, Paul, strikes a responsive cord in those who are living in the last half of life.

> . . . in his last days, Paulus was able to glimpse nonbeing. When he walked, a slim, white-haired wisp of a man now, over the lawn of his garden at the sea, Death watched him from the branches of every tree. Death silently enclosed him, whispering to him softly and pointing out a new borderline to be crossed. When he touched the leaves of his rhododendron bushes, still green and juicy, he knew he belonged to the other side. When he looked at the apples that had fallen from the tree, he knew they would soon be invisible to him. The knowledge of death came to him and he was able to weep about leaving this earth to enter nonbeing.[35]

No one will weep at the funeral of William Robert McClelland as I will. No one can know the miracle and uniqueness of my life—and, therefore, the utter tragedy and absurdity of its passing—as I do. When we begin to do the arithmetic of life in the second half, there is a certain sense of urgency about living it fully: a sense of "mustness." This "mustness" is born of the impatient little child who has been ignored for so long and, like the children at the airport, is irrepressibly alive and demanding of expression. This is our one and only chance to live! And the child within is restless to get on with it. To miss the chance is a great tragedy if not the unforgivable sin.

Olive Schreiner characterizes the point graphically:

> I have sometimes thought it would be a terrible thing if when death came to a man or woman, there stood about his bed, reproaching him, not for his sins, not for his crimes of commission and omission toward his fellow-men, but for the thoughts and the visions that had come to him, and which he, not for the sake of sensuous pleasure or gain, had thrust always into the background, saying "Because of my art, my love and my relations to my fellow-men shall never suffer; there shall be no loaf of bread less baked, no sick left untended, no present human creature's need of me left unsatisfied because of it." And then,

when he is dying, they gather round him, the things he might have incarnated and given life to—and would not. All that might have lived, and now must never live for ever, look at him with their large reproachful eyes—his own dead visions reproaching him; "Was it worth it? All the sense of duty you satisfied, the sense of necessity you labored under: should you not have violated it and given us birth?" It has come upon me so vividly sometimes that I have almost leaped out of bed to gain air—that suffocating sense that all his life long a man or a woman might live striving to do his duty and then at the end find it all wrong.[36]

The awareness of limits and wasted time that the mid-life crisis brings means we can take up a conscious stance with regard to our own inevitable mortality.

It is this mature insight that will protect us from slavishly following what the culture wants us to do and from squandering our time in seeking the approval of others by conforming to their rules . . . . "Take back your silly rules!" we can shout at last. "No one can dictate what is right for me . . . . For the fact is this is my one and only journey through life."[37]

A woman in the hospital was weeping after being told she was terminally ill with cancer. When a friend sought to console her she replied, "I'm not weeping because I'm dying. I'm weeping because I never lived." The woman understood the import of the poet's words,

I would rather be ashes than dust.
I would rather my spark should burn in a brilliant blaze
    than should be stifled in dry rot.
I would rather be a superb meteor,
    every atom of me in magnificent glow,
    than a sleepy and permanent planet.
Man's chief purpose is to live not to exist.[38]

Those lines are but a secular version of the more theological-sounding answer to the first question of the Westminster Catechism, "What is the chief purpose of human life?" The response: "The chief end of humankind is to glorify God, and enjoy her forever." To risk enjoying God in the second half of life by giving birth to those inner life urges that have been so long stifled, is to experience in a different sense the vision of Martin Luther King, Jr. "Free at last! Free at last! Great God Almighty, we are free at last!"

Such freedom costs something, of course. It means moving out of the rational and sane world of adulthood with the acquired values and assigned roles. It means trusting the urgings of the child within and risking the belief that he or she knows more about our life than others do.

There is a little child in all of us who has dreams to dream and places to go, people to see and things to do, a life to be explored. But the world is full of unimaginative, responsible people who say to that little child, "And what do you want to do when you grow up?"

The Dutch doctor who, late in life, left his practice, his family, and his friends to sail around the world by himself knew what he wanted to do. It took him sixty years, but he finally realized a boyhood dream. We may assume that his friends and family thought of him as irresponsible or in his second childhood. But I suspect Jesus might have said, "Of such is the kingdom of God."

The real question lingers, however, "What does your trip around the world look like?" What is that dream that has been put out of mind for the sake of the rules and regulations? What is that dream that the little child is longing to realize and of which Jesus says life and living is all about?

To believe in God is to be one of those kids who just refuses to grow up and get older, and older and older, and die forever. "Let the little child come to me," says Jesus, "And do not forbid him or her, for to such belongs the kingdom of God. Indeed I say to you, unless you become that little child, you cannot enter the Kingdom."

God Prefers Sinners

To risk giving birth to the child within, however, is to risk finding that the child is a prodigal. Luke tells the story of a young fellow who asked for a share of his father's estate, received it, and proceeded to spend it all on wine, women, and song (Luke 15:11-32). Like so many of the teachings of Jesus that the church has tamed to fit into its comfortable religious expectations, the church has taken Luke's story and called it "The Prodigal Son," the sinner who ran away from home and squandered his father's inheritance in loose living. But a sinner who *repented,* and because he *repented,* was able to come home and live again in his father's house. Unlike the adulterous woman in Nathaniel Hawthorne's *The Scarlet Letter,* who held her head high, the church sees the prodigal as one who was properly humbled and came home with head bowed. Having groveled in the pigsty, he came to his senses and, because he properly repented, said, "I am sorry." Then he was able to once again enjoy the good favor of his father.

But if that is what Jesus had in mind—that is, focusing on the prodigal, his sin and his repentance—why did Jesus include the irrelevant narrative of the almost forgotten elder brother?

Now his elder brother was in the field; and as he came and drew near to the house, he heard music and dancing. And he called one of the servants and asked what this meant. And he said to him, "Your brother has come, and your father has killed the fatted calf, because he has received him safe and sound." But he was angry and refused to go in. His father came out and entreated him, but he answered his father, "Lo, these many years I have served you, and I never disobeyed your command; yet you never gave me a kid, that I might make merry with my friends. But when this son of yours came, who has devoured your living with harlots, you killed for him the fatted calf!" (Luke 15:25-30)

The elder brother was a good fellow. There is no reason to paint him with the dark brush of self-righteousness as is frequently done. Jesus portrays this brother as the one who stayed home, worked hard, and was obedient to the father's commands. He upheld the family name loyally. He knew he had a claim to his father's favor because he had earned it. But he also knew that his younger brother had earned his father's good graces because he had repented of his sins. Repentance, like obedience, also earns grace. That may be bad theology, but functionally, we believe it—and practice it. The elder son had a claim on the father's favor by way of faithful obedience. Yet the younger brother also had a claim to his father's forgiveness by virtue of his change of heart. We believe God is gracious to forgive those who repent. So, if the point of the story is on sin and repentance, then the elder brother's reaction is out of place. His objection makes no sense.

But, no, the elder brother was angry because he sensed there was something ominously out of place in the way the father was responding to his prodigal brother. He sensed there was something inappropriate in the celebration of the return of the wanderer. It began to dawn on him that the father loved the sinner, not because he had repented, not because he had earned his forgiveness, not even in spite of his sin and rebelliousness but *because* of it. Jesus is telling a story that calls forth a response of righteous indignation in every good, self-respecting, church-attending, Bible-reading, religious person because the point of the story is that all of the celebration is born of the fact that God prefers—dare we say it?—God prefers sinners!

It is not that the prodigal was better looking or more talented than his elder brother. It was, rather, that he had learned something about life. He had discovered the relativity of rules and regulations. He had learned that life is not bound by Law. Life is a gift of Grace. Rules and regulations are human constraints. But life cannot be constrained by definitions and laws—even when they are laid on us by parents or society, the church or religion. The prodigal son had risked living. He had heard a different tune being played and had responded by dancing to the melody. He had discovered the absurd, sometimes humorous, but always haunting Piper who plays the song of life and is called the God of Grace. The younger brother had grasped the opportunity to live. He had *risked* it. To be sure, he had scars. He had known times of hunger and despair. He was covered with grime. He had hurt others and been hurt himself. But *he had lived.* No wonder the father preferred him. He had slides to show and a story to tell.

Such fullness of life is never understood by the elder brothers and sisters who live restricted, safe lives at home, bound by conventions and mores. Hannah Tillich, in her revealing auto-biography, tells of the far countries to which her husband, Paul, journeyed. Most of us would be shocked at the disclosures concerning Paul Tillich's life that she makes. Tillich: the world-renowned theologian and shaper of modern theology. Tillich: the prodigal son, lover of pornography and women, having affairs with students and secretaries!

There can be no doubt that Tillich was one of the great spokespersons for the God of Grace. During the 1960s, the decade of campus agnosticism, elder brothers were struggling with great difficulty to make sense of the Christian faith to that student generation. Yet Tillich was able to fill lecture halls and auditoriums when he spoke. Students sensed in him the pulse of life. They heard in him the Word of the Creator and Sustainer of life. They heard in that prodigal's theology the Word of Grace.

Where did the Word come from? Hannah, in assessing her husband's life says,

> He called on ecstasy as the tremulous instigator of sacred action. He dared open "the doors of the deep" to the monsters of his convulsed wishes and unfulfilled desires. By boldly naming them and showing their faces, he coined a new philosophical-theological language. Courageously, he pushed the image of God beyond the concept of heaven. By dematerializing and depersonalizing Him, he threw the weight of sin and grace back upon the human soul. He said "yes" to his own being.[39]

By saying yes to his own being, Tillich discovered the Word of God who is the Ground of Being. That is why the Father preferred the prodigal. He had said *yes* to the gift of life that had been given to him. Like Tillich, he had probed the possibilities and pushed the boundaries ever wider. If he had told his own story, he might have said, with Tillich,

> The boundary is the best place for acquiring knowledge. When I was asked to give an account of the way my ideas have developed from my life, I thought that the concept of the boundary might be the fitting symbol for the whole of my personal and intellectual development. At almost every point, I have had to stand between alternative possibilities of existence, to be completely at home in neither and to take no definitive stand against either.[40]

God wants us to live. But in order to say yes to life we must be able to live with the ambiguities within ourselves. The story that Jesus tells is not a plea that we become prodigals, though there is good news in it for those times when we are. But neither is there any reason to assume that the prodigal changed. He did not lose his wanderlust. There is no evidence to suggest that his genes were rearranged and his personality altered. He still was a lover of life, still had a hankering for good food, fine wine, and beautiful women. But he had been accepted *as he was.* Yes, there is good news for prodigals.

But the story is not a plea to become a prodigal because the story is not about the prodigal son. It is not about sin and repentance, as the church has assumed. It is, rather, a story that gives us permission to live with the amazing ambiguities within ourselves. It is about the Father and his radical acceptance of *both* sons. Both lived together under the same roof, and though they probably never understood one another, the story makes it clear that they were both members of one household, living there by the grace of the Father.

There are within all of us conflicting voices: members of our board of directors who speak from opposite sides of the table. Usually some of the members have been belittled or ignored over the years. Yet they have persisted. And rather than being intimidated by their louder, more tyrannical colleagues have, in fact, grown more insistent. Part of the distress, and hence the developmental task required of middle age, is coming to terms with all the members of our board—especially those with prodigal leanings. The good news, of which this story speaks, is that both brothers were accepted as part of one household. Our dignity, therefore, does not rest in our innocence, nor our shame in our guilt. Our dignity rests simply in the fact that God loves us as we are in all of our ambiguous and conflicting complexity. We are invited by the story to accept the reality of our situation: We have been accepted by the Grace of God and given permission to live our convoluted lives.

Guess Who's Coming to Dinner

The acceptance of us as we are, is the point of another story told by Luke; it is also about a questionable character (Luke 7:36-50). This time it is Simon the Pharisee, who has prepared the banquet for his distinguished guest, Jesus the mighty prophet.

The story begins in a thoroughly predictable manner. Simon, a good upstanding churchman, one of the best educated members of the community and no doubt a civic leader, invites the Distinguished Guest to dinner. What could be more natural? Simon probably came home, strutting, and announced to his wife, "Guess who's coming to dinner! Jesus of Nazareth, the holy man of God."

Probably all of us can reach back into our memories and pull out a similar incident when our parents invited the minister to dinner. Mother would bring out the best silver and table linen. We were instructed to be on our best behavior. The conversation was guarded—nothing too controversial—because, after all, the guest in our home was a holy man of God.

So the dinner that Simon the Pharisee planned was to be in every respect proper. But then there was this disturbance.

And behold, a woman of the city, who was a sinner, when she learned that [Jesus] was at table in the Pharisee's house, brought an alabaster flask of ointment, and standing behind him at his feet, weeping, she began to wet his feet with her tears, and wiped them with the hair of her head, and kissed his feet, and anointed them with the ointment. Now when the Pharisee who had invited him saw it, he said to himself, "If this man were a prophet, he would have known who and what sort of woman this is who is touching him, for she is a sinner." (Luke 7:37-39)

This, too, could have been predicted. After all, public figures are the targets of demonstrations. Even the President of the United States has his hecklers. You expect that sort of thing when riffraff is around. But what was unexpected, and indeed most disturbing to Simon, was Jesus' reaction. The Distinguished Guest did not seem to mind the interruption—nor her attention. No doubt Simon wondered who it was who had come to dinner. If a holy man could not recognize a sinner when he saw one, something must be terribly wrong. The woman made a spectacle of herself by falling all over Jesus and kissing his feet. Any of us, in a similar situation, would have been offended by all the touching. Certainly we would have felt awkward at being approached by this gushy, overpainted woman of the street. With studied composure and great benevolence, we might have responded with a clever putdown, such as, "My dear, go wash yourself." We would have expected Jesus to declare her behavior inappropriate, or at least to have disapproved of it by some sort of pained glance at Simon. But he did none of these things. He sat there accepting and—it would seem—enjoying all her attention.

Luke continues,

And Jesus answering said to him, "Simon, I have something to say to you." And he answered, "What is it, Teacher?" "A certain creditor had two debtors; one owed five hundred denarii, and the other fifty. When they could not pay, he forgave them both. Now which of them will love him more?" Simon answered, "The one, I suppose, to whom he forgave more." And he said to him, "You have judged rightly." Then turning toward the woman he said to Simon, "Do you see this woman? I entered your house, you gave me no water for my feet, but she has wet my feet with her tears

71

and wiped them with her hair. You gave me no kiss, but from the time I came in she has not ceased to kiss my feet. You did not anoint my head with oil, but she has anointed my feet with ointment. Therefore I tell you, her sins, which are many, are forgiven, for she loved much; but he who is forgiven little, loves little." And he said to her, "Your sins are forgiven." Then those who were at table with him began to say among themselves, "Who is this, who even forgives sins?" And he said to the woman, "Your faith has saved you; go in peace." (Luke 7:40-50)

Jesus tries to explain his action, or lack of same, to Simon by telling a story the point of which is that the gratitude of someone who has been forgiven much is obviously going to be greater than the appreciation of someone who has been forgiven a very little. The clear implication of the story is that this woman has a lot for which to be forgiven. She is certainly a sinner. No question about it. Far more of a sinner than Simon the Pharisee ever thought of being.

Here we come to the point of Luke's account. It is very interesting to note that this story is told in one form or another by all four of the Gospels. But when Mark tells the story, he focuses on the anointing with the costly perfume, thereby using it as an announcement of Jesus' death and burial. When John tells the story, he uses it to make Judas look bad. Matthew tells the story to make a statement about poor people. It is when we realize what the others did not say that Luke's point becomes all the more incredible. In Luke's narrative, Jesus knows full well what kind of woman this is and says, "Your sins are forgiven." For Luke's readers the question whether Jesus had the authority of God to forgive sins was a major concern. Luke, therefore, focuses his account on the issue of whether Jesus was really the Son of God who had the authority to forgive sins. Twenty centuries later that is no longer a major issue in the Christian church. We assume Jesus to be the Son of God and, therefore, has full power to forgive sins or retain them. So the significance of Luke's story is missed unless we ask the question, "What does it mean for Jesus to say to this sinful woman that her sins are forgiven?"

Functionally speaking, Jesus is saying, "Your sins don't matter. Your faith has saved you. Your sins have not closed you off from God because your faith—your vision of life, your sense of ultimate values, your ability to hope, your capacity to love—

has saved you from hardness of heart in a way in which Simon the Pharisee has not been saved. Your sins have not mattered. His relatively few sins have only served to insulate him from God. But your lifestyle has not blinded you to the miracle of grace. Go in peace."

What is conspicuously absent in this story are the words that would have made both Simon and the church feel a lot better, "Go and sin no more." But Jesus says nothing of this kind to the woman. He simply says, "Your sins have not separated you from God. They have not gotten in the way."

The Gospels contain a similar story of a woman taken in adultery. She was dragged before the court of the Pharisees who gathered around her, ready to administer the *coup de grace*. It was an open and shut case. She had been caught redhanded. She deserved the death penalty because she was a "sinful" woman, and the Law prescribed her punishment. But then this man who came to dinner entered the scene and simply said, "Let him who is without sin cast the first stone." The obvious implication was that none of them was sinless. After her would-be judges had slunk off for home, Jesus asked her, "Where are those who accuse you?" She looked up and replied, "Nowhere, my Lord." Jesus then said, "Neither do I accuse you." The story probably ended there, but the church could not rest comfortably with the conclusion so it tacked on the ending, "Go and sin no more." As such it is an absurd ending. "Go and sin no more" is an impossible command to lay on us as Jesus very well knew and as his words, "Let him who is without sin . . ." made clear. (See John 8:1-11.)

Returning to our story in Luke: Not only does Jesus not condemn the woman who anointed his feet, but he speaks of her in a commendable way, "Your faith has saved you." We can anticipate Simon's protest, "How could a sinful woman have a saving faith? What about my faith?" The Pharisee is absolutely correct in being disturbed. This is not what you would expect from a man of God! Luke has drawn us into the story and we now face a crisis of faith. Do we dismiss the Good News because it does not fit our religious expectations, or do we accept the Word on its own terms? Do we dismiss Christ as the Man of God because he does not measure up to our definition of what a savior should be, or do we set aside our preconceptions and receive the Man of Grace? What if God is a scandalous God? Do we then create a new God to worship?

The record is clear. Our God is a scandalous God. She visits this earth through the offspring of an unwed mother. She leaves this earth through the death of a man with a criminal record. She comes among us through the Holy Spirit in what the world perceives to be a drunken orgy. It is almost as though the Bible is saying you can always tell when God is around because there is the smell of scandal about her presence. So it is in this story. Sins do not matter. Blasphemy! The Pharisee concludes that Jesus is obviously not a holy man. Perhaps an imposter, but at best nothing more than a teacher; one among many, who can be taken or left alone, depending on whether or not you happen to agree with his teachings.

The sinful woman on the other hand, sees clearly: This man is the Holy One of God. In her experience—and she has had a lot of it—she has tasted both the good and the bad. She has long since given up trying to live by noble principles. Compromise has become a way of life. She is not a repentant sinner. She has not earned her forgiveness. She will be out on the streets tomorrow in the same way that she was yesterday and the day before. But she knows something. She knows that one cannot escape a sinful life. Whereas Simon lives in a mythical world of pure right and total wrong—a fantasy world in which one can escape sinfulness by a simple choice—the woman knows that all of living is tainted with sin. She is, therefore, willing to live; recklessly if necessary, but nevertheless willing to risk living.

Simon, on the other hand, lives very carefully. He lives thinking there is an area of life which is untainted by sin and in which he can be safe. He views life as a tightrope-walker, concentrating every moment on each step lest he topple off and be lost forever in the abyss. He focuses on his feet rather than the view. He must be very careful and cautious. His attention is riveted on what is right and what is wrong, what is good and what is evil. The Pharisee lives in a religious world of labels and distinctions, of definitions and rules, all of which must be kept in mind at all times to prevent falling into "sinful" living.

The woman lives in a different kind of reality. For her life is simply a given. There are no rules that are not relative. There are no absolutes. There are only functional definitions that make life more or less bearable.

Years ago when I was learning to fly, I had to practice takeoffs and landings. After one particularly awkward landing—just this side of a controlled crash—I commented in embarrassment to my instructor, "That was really a miserable landing." His reply contained the wisdom of the ages, "It's a good landing if you can walk away from it." In Luke's story, goodness is not some abstract concept; it is the ability to survive the landing and be amazed by life. Simon is concerned about whether or not it is a good or bad landing, a sinful or a righteous life. But the labels only make sense from his perspective. His definition of "sinful" fits only if you buy his assumption that it is important to label life and to live in a maze of distinctions.

As a result, the Pharisee sees Jesus not as the Christ but simply as a teacher, one whom you invite to dinner for interesting table conversation. You milk his mind for all you can get out of it. Then you say, "Wasn't that a lovely and interesting evening?" But the woman, the "sinful" woman, is amazed at something *new* in her life. She has encountered total goodness and she sees the encounter as something fragile, something never to be encountered again, a once-in-a-lifetime event. She sees Jesus not as a teacher but as the Precious One.

For his part, Jesus sees her as a beautiful and successful human being because she has survived. She can feel in a way that Simon cannot feel. She has survived, not nobly perhaps, nor sinlessly. But she can love. She can laugh and cry. She can give herself recklessly, touchingly, lovingly to life. She can see miracles of Grace to which Simon is blind.

And there the story ends. There is no moral drawn for us. But the Gospel narrative is powerful in its judgment. She is alive. Simon is dead. In his fascination with flawed living, he is in danger of missing the whole magnificent parade. It is a problem for religiously oriented people who feel that the distinctions between right and wrong, good and evil are crucial for successful living. But as we have seen, Jesus does not require sinless living. If we are to risk living fully, therefore, it is imperative that we move beyond our neurotic need to make such distinctions. One of the great difficulties we have in attaining the free flight of middle age is breaking through the sound barrier of our compulsive fixation on sinfulness. The Gospel of John relates a story that hooks into our obsession.

Believing Is Seeing

As [Jesus] passed by, he saw a man blind from his birth. And his disciples asked him, "Rabbi, who sinned, this man or his parents, that he was born blind?" Jesus answered, "It was not that this man sinned, or his parents, but that the works of God might be made manifest in him." (John 9:1-3)

"Who sinned?" How typical for our attention to be focused on the faults in people's lives. And how accustomed we are to thinking our afflictions are due to our sin! It is not unusual for religion to connect sin and suffering as though the latter were a mistake in the grand design of things. How typically American to assume that virtue earns its own rewards and that evil is punished.

Suffering serves a purpose in the scheme of things. It is part of our intellectualization of life. It fills in the blanks so that everything fits and makes sense. The connection between sin and suffering allows us to process the data of life in a meaningful manner. The blind man, therefore, had earned his keep. He had paid his dues to society. He was living testimony, for the relief of all, that good guys win and bad guys lose.

Jesus' reply, therefore, is exceedingly subversive. "No one sinned." The man's blindness has nothing to do with sin. No connection. Talk of sin is totally irrelevant for understanding this situation. If a reason is needed to make sense of it, Jesus suggests that it be understood as a vehicle for God's power to be made known. The man's *blindness* is the occasion for people to *see* God at work.

Clearly, therefore, this is not a story of reprimand or judgment. Nor is it a healing story, even though Jesus opens the man's eyes and gives him sight. The man had been born blind. That was his *natural* state of being: blind. He is not healed therefore, but he is changed. The distinction is crucial for those going through the changes of mid-life. Our condition, as was true of the blind man, is radically altered by God's intervention. We are getting older, but that fact alone renders our situation pregnant with possibilities. John is asking us to view this man's blindness as the natural condition with which God worked. We are thereby invited to look at our present situation and see it as the arena in which God encounters us, changes us, and enables us to see life in a radically different way. She wants us to see her as God, and ourselves as citizens of her kingdom, a realm that is spread all around us—middle-aged crazy and all—but only for those who have eyes to see and ears to hear.

As presented by John, therefore, it is our story. Jesus announces that the kingdom of God is at hand. We are to repent and believe the good news.

The call for repentance is not to be understood from the perspective of our fixation on sin as if it were a denunciation of moral failures. It is not to be translated, "Knock off your naughtiness and shape up." Rather it is a call to turn around. We are looking in the wrong direction for life, and as a result we are blind. Turn around and *see* that life is to be understood not by what has been but by what can be. Look at life differently. Try another perspective. Try believing, for believing is seeing things as they really are. Turn around and believe the good news of the Kingdom's presence. To repent and believe, therefore, is to see what is present in the upheavals and restlessness of our lives. We are to understand what is happening in these mid-life changes. We are not freaks nor are we deserting the faith. Rather, the kingdom of the God of Grace is upon us.

The Bible invites us to risk believing God loves us as we are. Look at the story. The man was born blind. Blindness was a natural fact of his being. There was no moral judgment attached to it. He was just blind. God did not require him to see in order to be loved. Seeing was not a precondition for acceptance. The good news of the Kingdom of Grace is that we do not have to do *anything* to enter it. We need only believe it. We are in it. We do not need to shape up. We do not have to get our act together. We can come with all of our abilities and inabilities. God accepts us as we are—radically and unconditionally. We do not have to first forgive our enemies to get in, or have a proven prayer record. To get in we do not have to be more loving or to leave behind our jealousies or neuroses. We do not have to leave anything behind. God's radical acceptance takes us where we are and as we are. She accepts us in our blindness.

This amazing love of God is so hard to accept because both the American way and the religious way assume we must earn it and somehow be worthy of it. Especially is this true when, in the turbulence of the mid-life journey, we feel confused about values and beliefs once held sacred and seem strangers not only to the person in the bathroom mirror but to God as well.

So Jesus' admonition is for us the more urgent. Repent and believe! Turn around, middle-aged Americans, you are looking in the wrong direction. This is not some capitalistic grace that you can buy. Turn around, religious church-going people. This is not something that makes sense of your righteousness or wickedness. Repent and believe! Try believing that the strangeness of your passage is God's idea, and see what happens to your vision.

When we begin to *believe,* the first thing we *see* is that we are accepted radically, unconditionally, as we are. There is nothing we can ever do that will change God's decision to love us. It is not that we are once accepted but thereafter must walk a tightrope of obedience to stay acceptable. No! There is nothing any one of us can ever do that will make the God of Grace blink. No matter how clumsy we may be at navigating the currents of middle age.

But more important, our vision enables us to see beyond what is, to what can be. God wants us to become new creatures. This is the second thing we see in the Kingdom of Grace. God's love moves beyond the concept of mere acceptance. She loves us the way we are, but her intention is for us to see and not be forever blind.

To use the analogy of romantic love: I have learned over the course of many married years that to love my wife means I love her not only for the person she is but for the person she is becoming. It is often said that love is blind. But in fact, love is amazingly clear of sight. It sees with the eyes of grace. It sees what the other person can become. My spouse is a growing, developing, ever-changing person. If I am to love her as God loved this blind man, then I must give up my neurotic need for her to remain as she was when I first met her. She does not exist to fulfill my needs. Rather I exist to help her become all that she can be, by the grace of God. To be a good mate is for me to be a good steward of her becoming.

It is a common complaint among married people to say, "You're not the person I married." But what is really being said is, "I married you, dear, for comfort and security, thinking you would meet my needs and I would meet yours. I assumed we would settle down, hang out our marital shingle, 'Business as Usual,' and live happily ever after." Many couples hold such a view. It is a common understanding of love and marriage.

But there is a deeper level of understanding marital commitment. To free the other person from my needs is a consummation devoutly to be wished—at least by God. We let go of our mates and free them from a grasping, essentially selfish love, and we come to love them for who they are becoming. *Their* becoming has very little to do with *our* needs. Marital commitment does not mean I bind my spouse to a list of specific expectations until death do us part. Marital commitment means: I intend to share with my spouse, for life, the great adventure of living and help her grow and become all that she can become, even though it occasionally hurts and ignores some of my needs. Obviously, such an understanding of commitment and love, based as it is on becoming new creatures by God's grace, can be detrimental to the comfort and peace of marriage as many in our society conceive it. This brings us back to our story.

God meets us where we are, but her design is to lead us along the path to greater wholeness. Such activity by God is, traditionally, called Grace. But miracles of Grace, as we noted earlier, usually disrupt our nice, tidy systems and can cause, as they did in this case, massive hostility.

Now it was a sabbath day when Jesus made the clay and opened his eyes . . . . Some of the Pharisees said, "This man is not from God, for he does not keep the sabbath." But others said, "How can a man who is a sinner do such signs?" There was a division among them. (John 9:14, 16)

Miracles of Grace have an unnerving way of reminding us there is more to life than can be contained in our systems of religious beliefs, law, or morality. Life is bigger than our commitments, bigger than any existing relationship. To become a new creature and have our eyes opened can be terribly threatening to the order we have established and the relationships we have taken for granted. This can constitute the blindness that makes sense and feels comfortable but that keeps us from seeing the Kingdom. Then Jesus comes into our cozy blindness and opens our eyes. We see. Our order is threatened. Foundations are shaken. The earth trembles and life is viewed differently. Nothing is the same.

The third aspect, therefore, that we come to see about the Kingdom is that living in it is awkward. Kingdom living is a state of being that is betwixt and between. We are caught between the blind system, which gives structure and stability to life, and the graceful state of seeing that no system of beliefs or morality can hold all of life. What were thought to be absolutes chiseled in granite are now seen in all of their relativity, yet stubbornly remaining as influences with which we must deal.

Christians, like the blind man who now sees, are an enigma to those around them. They are condemned to live awkwardly, clumsily, making mistakes, not knowing whether it is proper to be in the old world or the new one, stumbling sometimes, but always risking. Disciples know they can never go back to their blindness because, by grace, they now see.

To live in the Kingdom is a little like rock climbing. We climb up to a ledge and look down. We are terrified. We look up and are sure we can go no higher. There we are on our ledge, not knowing how to proceed. One thing only is certain; we cannot go down. But neither can we stay on our ledge forever. There is only one alternative: We must risk awkwardly climbing higher. The only way to go is up. Growth is always upsetting, and Christ's coming radically disorients us because we see the kingdom of God all around us, with all of its possibilities, yet are not quite sure what to do with them.

Howard Thurman shares a delightful account of a child just learning to walk. In the process the child grabs a tablecloth and pulls himself up. The tablecloth is pulled off the table and all of the dishes come crashing to the floor.

Of course the child cannot grasp his mother's reaction to his behavior. It must be very puzzling indeed. But he cannot be put off. Another time comes. With a fresh start he finally makes the upright position. Behold him now! There he is, suspended between ceiling and floor with his little feet touching; his entire body shouts, "I did it! I did it!" Then the floor rises up to meet him. But he has established for one prophetic moment his independence of his environment. He has made the crucial physical distinction between the self and the not-self. The meaning of physical distance is experienced. He stands unsupported and alone, an autonomous object in the midst of a world of objects, and there is *room* for movement between them. The peculiar place of the self is established—never quite to be lost again.[41]

Once we have stood in the peculiar place of Grace and seen the Kingdom, we know we can never be the same. We live in the Kingdom with laughter at the absurdity and amazement of it all and with tears for its awkwardness and pain. We live betwixt and between, sometimes more in the one world than the other, but knowing the difference.

The divine madness of life has given us radical permission to live. In so believing, we see the kingdom of God, a kingdom in which we are radically accepted now and forever as we are—no matter what, a Kingdom in which God is calling us—through those inner urges of life pulsating deep within—to become all that we can be. If we believe the disruptions and the awkwardness that come with middle age are of God, middle age can be a time of such seeing. Such believing is an act of courage on our part. The seeing is a gift of grace.

Chapter Four

A Bifocal Vision of Kingdom Living

Faith Stages Along Life's Way

Middle age can be a time when both life and God are seen in a totally different way. Fortunately, or unfortunately, we do not embark on the mid-life journey at the same time. As a result, what is seen clearly by one person may not be by another. Indeed, your new understanding may be quite threatening to me if I have not seen or experienced what you have. Jesus' understanding of God often confused his listeners because they did not share his vision. They were at a different stage of faith development than he. The result was, for Jesus, as well as his followers, frustrating to say the least.

> Jesus said to them, " . . . Do you not yet perceive or understand? Are your hearts hardened? Having eyes do you not see, and having ears do you not hear? And do you not remember? . . . Do you not yet understand?" (Mark 8:17, 18, 21)

Apparently, understanding takes time, and the simple truth is that some have lived longer and understand more than others. We are spread out along a continuum of experience that either predisposes us to recognize the God of Grace or prevents us from seeing him.

Lawrence Kohlberg has done some pioneering research in examining this continuum as it relates to moral development. At the risk of oversimplifying his work, let me summarize his views.

Kohlberg sees us beginning with a very self-centered understanding of life, a "me first" attitude toward others. Some of us move through this stage and come to see that other people also have needs. At this somewhat more advanced stage of our development, we can hear their pleas and be concerned with human rights and social justice. We are able to consider resolving our claims in relation to their rights. "An eye for an eye and a tooth for a tooth" seems a reasonable guide to behavior.

Self-sacrificing love is yet a further stage in moral development. In it, we are able to put others first. A parent's love for children usually transcends justice and fair play and centers on the needs and well-being of the offspring. The love of one marriage partner for another often achieves this level of maturity.

Quite clearly, a person at a more developed stage of moral understanding will have difficulty trying to communicate with a person in an earlier stage. It will be an exercise in frustration, if not futility. For a teacher like Jesus to call his listeners to love their enemies when they are in the self-centered stage is to invite confusion and misunderstanding, if not outright disagreement. As a result, Jesus often said cryptically at the end of his sermons, "He who has ears to hear, let him hear."

Similarly, there are stages through which a growing faith moves as it progresses along life's way. The first stage of faith development is that of a child. Probably one of the earliest words we heard as a youngster was "No"—more probably, "No, no, no!" Sometimes we heard words of praise from our parents, "Good boy" or "Good girl." Because we wanted to please, we learned what it took to fit into their expectations. Amplifying the point, we learned to live in a community of people—a society—with all of its "shoulds" and "oughts." In the child stage of faith development, therefore, the Law looms large. It is a primary concern. Jesus is seen as the great moral teacher who lays down prescriptions that enable us to please God, to get to heaven and escape hell. In this first stage of our faith development, obedience to God's will, as revealed in the Law, is of crucial importance and disobedience a major fear.

Most of us go through a second stage of development when we become rebels. In this stage we drop out of religion. Religion is "old hat," the church something we have outgrown. We know all of *that* or, more likely, we know better than *that*. In the rebel stage, we are aware of ourselves as over against the Law and its requirements of "shoulds" and "oughts." We test the limits. We resist authority because it is there. Discipline is an anathema precisely because it is discipline. Our rebellion is a sometimes awkward assertion of our newly developed self-identity. It is a matter of principal to oppose the authority of God, the church, and religion.

Of course, we can get stuck in any of these stages of developing faith. But if we successfully navigate the passage through the rebel stage, we come to a third stage: that of the adult. The adult again looks at the old religion that was jettisoned and finds that, in fact, it represents real experience and contains great wisdom. There is truth embedded in its archaic formulations and rituals, and though the truth needs to be reworded and refined, there is "gold in them thar hills." The adult stage is the time when we evaluate the various truth claims and find our own answers. We weigh wisdom. We choose the myths and stories by which we shall live. The adult knows it is not a question of living or not living by faith. It is only a question of choosing by which faith to live.

No wonder people heard Jesus so differently. Some heard him as the wise counselor, teacher, and friend. They listened to him gladly. Others heard Jesus as a divine guru who had the power of God. They followed him obediently. Still others heard Jesus as a tyrannical hypocrite with a messianic complex. They resisted his invitation to discipleship.

These three stages of faith development would alone account for the kind of confusion that frustrated Jesus. But there are more. The stage beyond the adult is what Keen calls the "outlaw." This stage of faith development begins with a crime, and it cuts the umbilical cord linking us to all of the old authorities. Ancient Greek mythology portrayed it in the person of Prometheus, who stole fire from the gods. The Old Testament presents the outlaw stage in the story of Adam and Eve, who transcended the limitations placed on them by God and ate the forbidden fruit. Their eyes were opened and—like God—they knew good and evil. Jesus embodies the outlaw stage when, after having been raised in the tradition of Jewish regard for the Torah, he disregarded the law by making it relative to human needs. His healing activities on the Sabbath come to mind, as does the time he and his disciples walked through a wheat field on a Sabbath day, gathered some grain, threshed it in their hands, and ate it. When the Pharisees accused him, Jesus said, "The law was made for people, not people for the law." (See Mark 2:27.)

Dietrich Bonhoeffer and the Berrigan brothers offer more contemporary examples of the outlaw stage of faith development. Each of them, in their own way, realized that certain ethical situations and the requirements of responsibility could not be covered by religious or civil law. Therefore, they were willing to assume the guilt of participating in acts of disobedience in the name of a higher authority. The outlaw stage of faith development is not characterized by resisting authority for the sake of rebelling, as was true in the rebel stage. Unlike the rebel, the outlaw is not merely testing the limits for the sake of testing the limits. Rather, the outlaw has discovered that no law is absolute and that all authority is relative. Therefore, the outlaw is simply not overly concerned about living within them.

The prodigal son was an outlaw. His elder brother who stayed at home and lived by his father's law, never questioning nor testing it, was still in the child stage. He had not yet grown through the rebelliousness of adolescence, nor did he live with the confidence of adulthood, since he had not internalized his father's values. The prodigal, on the other hand, had discovered that parental authority, and the values or morality of home, are not absolute. He had discovered a truth of greater significance: God alone is absolute—the God who stirs within us through those Easter urgings and calls us to live. The prodigal had discovered that God alone was Lord of his conscience. God wants no system of law or belief to come between himself and us; that is why he prefers outlaws.

Often this stage of faith development is ushered in by the mid-life crisis. The value of this time of life is that it is a growth period that provides a bridge from one stage of development to another. Neither religion nor the church, not to mention our society, are accustomed to thinking of the mid-life crisis in these terms. Anne Morrow Lindbergh wonders,

> Is it not possible that middle age can be looked upon as a period of second flowering, second growth, even a kind of second adolescence? It is true that society in general does not help one accept this interpretation of the second half of life. And therefore this period of expanding is often tragically misunderstood. Many people never climb above the plateau of forty-to-fifty. The signs

that presage growth, so similar, it seems to me, to those in early adolescence: discontent, restlessness, doubt, despair, longing, are interpreted falsely as signs of decay. In youth one does not as often misinterpret the signs; one accepts them, quite rightly, as growing pains. One takes them seriously, listens to them, follows where they lead. One is afraid. Naturally. Who is not afraid of pure space—that breath-taking empty space of an open door? But despite fear, one goes through to the room beyond.[42]

The mid-life crisis may not be an unmixed blessing, but the message contained in the stories and faith statements of scripture offers us a chance to understand those shifting sands of middle age as God's call to us. We are beckoned to move from the adult stage of our growing faith to yet a larger view of God's kingdom: the view of the outlaw. We are invited to see the relativity of authority and law and to trust the Kingdom call that stirs within. That call is characterized by a sense of urgency, by a sense of "must-ness." Responding to the call carries with it a certain sense of anxiety because growth means trusting the authority within rather than those external authorities that have claimed our allegiance before.

Eda LeShan finds an analogy in the lowly lobster:

In order to make the most of this new crisis of self-discovery in middle age, one has, in a sense, to become a lobster—only *knowing* the danger, which I presume lobsters are happily free from experiencing! In order to fit into his shell as he grows bigger, the lobster goes through periodic sheddings of his shell. During these times he is naked and vulnerable and in terrible danger of being eaten by his enemies in the sea. And yet, in the inexorability of nature, he must go through the crisis of dangerous exposure, or not grow. So with middle age, it is possible to remain stationary, to accept life as one has lived it and to settle for more of what has been, good and bad, and indifferent. One says, in effect, "Here I am in my middle age shell; I know myself quite well, where I am right now; life has its ups and downs, but I think I'll settle for what I know. It's the safe way, and I feel ready to be safe."[43]

LeShan underlines for us the point: There is nothing automatic about a growing faith. We can stall out and settle for the status quo. Clearly, some outgrow the old shells and some do not. We are not all at the same level in our development. This is why, in the early church, some believers were fanatically concerned about issues of Law. Circumcision, for example, was considered by them to be a prerequisite for becoming a Christian. Others saw no point in the ritual and never gave it a second thought. The former were the champions of law and order and concerned about the protocol of God. The latter, including the Apostle Paul, were dancing with the outlaw God of Grace and had not the slightest interest in the jots and tittles of legalistic niceties. No doubt Paul saw the members of the circumcision party as clods. And probably they saw him as irresponsible and immoral. The two parties were simply at different stages of their faith development.

There would seem to be an apparent conflict between the outlaw God of Grace and the God of Law; the Lord of the Dance and the Demander of Obedience. The conflict has led some theologians—Marcion, for example, in the early church—to conclude that there are two Gods: one spoken of in the Old Testament, the other revealed in the New. However, in Christ this apparent contradiction is resolved. Jesus said simply, "Think not that I have come to abolish the law and the prophets; I have come not to abolish them but to fulfil them" (Matt. 5:17).

It is not that the law is antagonistic to Christ and what he is about. But neither can the law contain nor comprehend the more complete disclosure of God in Christ. Obedience to the Law, therefore, cannot be the final word. Jesus Christ is that final Word made flesh. He reveals the Great Dancer of life; the God of Grace. Christ comes not to do away with the Law but to move us beyond it and, consequently, to fulfill its function.

The external authority of the Law functions as a scaffold in the building of life. It is the means, but relationship with God is the end. To remove the scaffold prematurely is destructive. But to leave it standing when it is no longer needed is suffocating. The mid-life crisis signals the time of dismantling. It is the *kairos*. It is the time of birthing. It is the time for accepting the invitation of the God of Grace to dance to a new tune, to trust him rather than the structure of Law. Not all of Jesus' listeners were middle aged of course. And not all of those who had garnered the experiences of those years were willing to risk trusting the inner voice. Thus Jesus would say poignantly, "I have yet many things to say to you, but you cannot bear them now" (John 16:12).

These words of Jesus seem to suggest there is yet another stage of development for faith—a fifth stage. Mystics and saints speak of it. Jesus lived in it. Let us call it the domain of the lover and the fool. There is not much I can say about it: First, because I do not know much about it yet myself, and what I do know has been gained by a little experience and a lot of hearsay. But a more significant reason for not saying too much about it is because silence is the vehicle for conveying its wisdom. Howard Thurman observed a few months before his death that wisdom is to know that most of what is worth saying can only be shared in silence.

To live in the land of the lovers and fools is to no longer be concerned with the question, "Who am I?" The lover has discovered the miracle of his or her own being and is amazed by it. But the discovery opens the lover to the miracle that exists in others. Concern for social justice and human rights stems, therefore, not from a principle of fair play or a vision of a new society, but from a genuine and deep appreciation of the sacredness of personhood.

The lover is also a fool. The fool no longer sees life as a problem to be understood nor a mystery to be solved. The fool looks at life, sometimes weeping, sometimes laughing. The same data cause both responses. Life is absurd and makes no sense, the fool knows this and has given up trying to understand it. Yet the fool is delighted and amazed by it. The only responses which are appropriate, therefore, are laughter at the absurdity of life and weeping at its incongruity. But above all, the fool embraces the whole of it and flows with its current: trusting life rather than fighting it.

There is a marvelous Zen story that characterizes life as a Buddhist monk running away from a killer tiger. The monk comes to the edge of a cliff with the hungry tiger in hot pursuit. Fortunately, the monk spies a vine growing over the cliff. He grabs hold of it and begins to climb down the cliff, out of the tiger's reach, who is by now glaring at him from above. But, lo, as the monk is climbing down, he looks and sees below him another ferocious tiger waiting, circling impatiently at the bottom of the cliff. To make matters worse, out of the corner of one eye the monk spies a mouse on a ledge above him, already beginning to gnaw the vine in two. Out of the corner of his other eye, the monk sees a strawberry growing from the rock. So he plucks the strawberry and eats it.

Trusting life is not belief that everything will turn out all right. Trust is daring to eat the strawberries which life provides. To trust God is to see life's beauty, not its sense; its gifts, not its happy endings; the miracle of it all, not the need to be in charge of it.

The lover and the fool live in the Now, neither enslaved by the past nor invested in the future. They live each moment, savoring its uniqueness and gracefulness. They do not seek to nail life down but rather flow with it. They dance to its varied tunes and trust both its gifts and the Giver who bestows them. They have learned to eat and enjoy the strawberries along the way. The poet Blake catches the spirit in these lines,

> He who bends to himself a joy
> Does the winged life destroy;
> But he who kisses the joy as it flies
> Lives in eternity's sunrise.[44]

The lover and the fool experience life as a joy and a gift of grace. They do not place demands on it. They neither clutch it in the belief that without their activity the world will not be properly shaped, nor do they try to make the world conform to some set of specifications. The world is not a place to be shaped by their well-intentioned involvement and action. It is rather the place for bearing witness to the miracle of life. Their concern for the world, its people, and its problems is boundless, but responsibility for the outcome of their efforts to change it belongs entirely to God. Everything matters, but nothing matters.

More than this I cannot say. Perhaps I have already said too much. Words can be inexact as well as misleading. Indeed, what I have said may make little sense. No matter! We are pilgrims who progress along the way, discovering wonder upon wonder, and every wonder true. The astounding privilege of living is given to us in day-tight compartments and its wisdom packaged in small insights. Grace is that vision of the Kingdom given to us along the way as we stumble and march, laugh and cry, succeed and fail, live and die.

But one thing is clear: there is yet room—even in middle age—to grow and develop. We are not fully mature until we have become fools and lovers, created in the image of a graceful God. This is probably why Jesus put so much emphasis on loving recklessly, that is, with total abandon, foolishly. He summarized our obligation before life in terms of love.

You shall love the Lord your God with all your heart, and with all your soul, and with all your mind, and with all your strength. . . . You shall love your neighbor as yourself. There is no other commandment greater than these. (Mark 12:30, 31)

The fact of the matter is, we are called to be lovers. Jesus directs us to love God with our whole *being* and to love our neighbor as we love *ourselves*. And although it is not always apparent, Jesus grounded our love of God and neighbor in the love of self: being . . . ourselves.

The Courage to Be

The New Testament is very clear about what love of neighbor means. In the parable of the Good Samaritan, it is evident that wherever human need is seen, there will be found the neighbor in need of loving. Unfortunately, the Bible is not as clear about what love of self means. Indeed, by the time Paul wrote his letter to the church at Rome, he was already imploring his readers not to think of themselves more highly than they ought to think (Rom. 12:3), and Luke was quoting Jesus, "If any man would come after me, let him deny himself and take up his cross daily and follow me" (Luke 9:23). Very early in the history of the church, a personal piety of self-denial came into vogue. Love of neighbor was understood as antithetic to love of self. Taking up our cross daily and following Jesus came to mean emptying ourselves of all personal pride, ambition, and self-worth, in order to obey God's command to love and serve others. Loving others was to be done at the expense of loving ourselves. "Greater love has no man than this, that a man lay down his life for his friends," Jesus was quoted as saying (John 15:13). Early Christian spirituality developed an individual ethic of self-sacrifice for the sake of others, and organized religion has been influenced by it ever since.

Theologically, what is at issue in this personal piety of self-sacrifice is that when we focus on the neighbor before we have fully come to appreciate ourselves, we cannot really love the neighbor. If we try to love our neighbor before we have come to realize the *miracle* of our own being and are amazed by it, love of neighbor inevitably becomes one of two things: either an irksome duty or a copout for living our own life, in which we overidentify with the other person. Either we love the neighbor because it is an obligation laid upon us by a judging God, and we do it in order to score brownie points, thereby earning heaven's reward; or we find ourselves living our lives vicariously through others and calling it "love of neighbor."

There are also psychological ramifications to such a piety. We can lose our identity. I once visited a patient in a psychiatric ward in a hospital. She was a model mother and a devoted wife. She lived for her family and her husband. That was her problem. She was so involved with the lives of her family, she forgot to live her own life. She was so caught up in their identities she was in danger of losing her own. She so valued them she no longer valued herself. Finally her unconscious mind rebelled. It literally threw a fit. The medical profession called it a nervous breakdown. It said, "Enough! It is time that you paid attention to yourself." And not until she did, did she begin to get well.

The problem with becoming selfless is that we become empty. Yet religion would have us not only lose our self-identity, but become little imitations of Jesus. "What would Jesus do?" is a popularized way of putting the ethical question, but it successfully does away with our selfhood in the process. Never mind that we have no idea what Jesus would do in the complex interrelationships of today's technological society. Never mind that the question is simplistic. The fact of the matter is Jesus never required his disciples to become like him. He loved and honored their uniqueness. He cherished their diversity. He did not try to iron out their idiosyncrasies; he saw them as gifts.

Peter had a spitfire temper and the impetuosity of a schoolboy. A psychiatrist would have said, "That's going to be a problem for a church leader. Better get some counseling or not enter the ministry." But Jesus looked at his neurosis and said, "It is a rock. I'm going to build a church on it." (Cf. Matt. 16:18.)

In 1933 Carl Jung observed, in his book *Modern Man in Search of a Soul,* "It is no easy matter to live a life that is modeled on Christ, but it is unspeakably harder to live one's own life as truly as Christ lived his." The question for Christians living today is not "What would Jesus do?"; for he has left us here not to live his life but our own. That is unspeakably more difficult. No one can do my living for me, or dying either, for that matter. God has not given my life to you, nor your life to someone else. No one but you will be held accountable for it. Jesus' summons to love is an invitation to value fully our own unique selves. It is not a call to selflessness. It is rather a call to self-affirmation. Only in loving ourselves and discovering the amazing miracle of our own being can we then love and be amazed at the miracle of another' being.

It is as if a seed were planted in each one of us at our conception. Encoded in its genetic structure a special identity is written. It blossoms into the unique life to which our name has been given. There are no two of us alike. Therefore, emptying ourselves and becoming selfless is blasphemous to the Creator God who went to a lot of trouble creating an infinite variety of human beings, each with his or her own individuality.

What is needed is not a reaffirmation of the selfless piety which suffocates our individuality but a new piety of self-affirmation. Friedrich Nietzche spoke of slave morality and master morality. A slave morality adopts values and follows a morality which is imposed upon us from beyond ourselves. A master morality, on the other hand, sees the self as the creator of values and morality. It, therefore, affirms the self. Nietzsche saw Christianity as the great espouser of slave morality because it portrayed values and morals as absolutes given by God. To the extent that this is true, human response can only be discussed in terms of obedience and disobedience to the divine will. Nietzsche contended that to be fully human is to realize morality is something we create. Values are not hung "out there" like stars in the sky. We are the ones who do the valuing.

It takes courage to affirm this realization, for it means affirming ourselves. To take responsibility for choosing the values and morals by which we live is always risky and, therefore, frightening. It is not likely that many will risk it without the experience and urgency of half a lifetime. But Jesus calls his followers to risk this kind of courage when he says,

No longer do I call you servants, for the servant does not know what his master is doing; but I have called you friends, for all that I have heard from my Father I have made known to you (John 15:15).

No longer are we to be slaves. We are to be friends with the master.

There are probably few words in all scripture that are more loaded than these. Jesus' words are all the more explosive because they appear so innocent. "You are my friends." How nice, we think, to be a friend of Jesus, to run in the best circles, to have connections in high places. There are certain privileges that go with being a friend of Jesus that have not gone unnoticed in the hymn,

> What a friend we have in Jesus,
> All our sins and griefs to bear!
> What a privilege to carry
> Everything to God in prayer![45]

Yet, less than twenty-four hours after Jesus designated the disciples as friends, they were running scared. Not one of them wanted to be known as a friend of Jesus. It was too risky. Far better to be a servant. Far better to live by a slave morality than to live as a friend of the Master. There is, after all, a certain security in being a servant. A servant cannot be blamed for the actions of the Master. A servant simply reports for duty and carries out orders. A servant does not have to think. There is no confusion. A servant bears no responsibility and takes neither credit nor blame. It was a defense heard often at the Nuremberg trials.

We can understand the anxiety that overtook the Hebrews after they had been delivered from their captivity. It produced an identity crisis. Forty years of maturing in the wilderness were required before they were ready to assume their new identity as God's people and take responsibility for their freedom. It took four decades to develop the necessary trust in the God of Grace. After years of bondage they were used to taking orders. None of them had ever needed to think before. As slaves they took no responsibility for themselves.

In the wilderness, condemned by God to freedom, they began to complain, "Moses, what have you done to us, bringing us out into the wilderness to die? It would have been far better if you had left us in Egypt as slaves. There, at least, we were taken care of. But out here in the wilderness, as free people, we have to live by trust in God and that's too risky." Freedom and maturity demand a price. So also does equality with Jesus.

Middle age means it is time to be friends with Jesus, not his servants. We long for the security of the slave because it simplifies our relationship to God. We simply live by the Law. Servants may obey or disobey the commands of their Master, but at least there is no confusion about what is required, and they always have the option of seeking the Master's forgiveness when they fail. The great privilege about which the church has so often spoken is God's forgiveness made available to repentant sinners. He makes everything right.

But when Jesus summarizes the law, he lays the emphasis upon our being: Love God with our whole being, he says, and then love our neighbor as we love our own being. His summary makes clear the difference between the piety of a servant and that of a friend. The piety of a servant hinges upon obedience or disobedience to God, and in disobedience the servant can hope for forgiveness. But the piety of being a friend means we must accept the responsibility for our own life as Jesus accepted responsibility for his. Consequently the clues to ethical behavior come from ourselves, not from God. Values are not prescribed for us, despite the claims of religion. They come rather from knowing ourselves. By listening to ourselves, our wants, our desires, our needs, as they begin to bubble to the surface from the unconscious, we begin to know what is really valued by us.

By middle age we are ready to trust those promptings. In our youth those inner stirrings, those hunches, those needs and wants are easily ignored. But by middle age they begin to express themselves with an urgency, a sense of mustness that can no longer be denied. These stirrings are what Glenn Clark used to speak of as "the soul's sincere desire." First we listen to them, then we can begin to trust them, for these stirrings speak with wisdom. They tell us what is crucial for our lives to be whole and good.

Interestingly, in the Gnostic *Gospel of Thomas* Jesus is reported to have said,

That which you have [within you] will save you if you bring it forth from yourselves. That which you do not have within you will kill you if you do not have it within you.[46]

Apparently, in Jesus' thinking, it was crucial that we listen to our deep yearnings—"the soul's sincere desire." In the *Dialogue of the Savior,* also one of the Gnostic documents discovered at Nag Hammadi, Jesus talks with three of his disciples. Matthew asks Jesus to show him the source of life. Where, he wonders, is the pure light to be found? Jesus answers, "Every one [of you] who has known himself has seen it."[47] When the disciples, expecting Jesus to reveal some deep secret to them, ask, "Who is the one who seeks [and who is the one who] reveals?" he answers, "the one who seeks [is also the one who] reveals."[48] The disciple who comes to know himself, therefore, can discover what even Jesus cannot teach.

This deep, inner wisdom is of God. The Bible itself invites us to think of God in terms of ourselves. It does so by speaking of humankind being created in the image of God. To say we are created in God's image is to say, at the very least, that knowing ourselves gives us the best clue to knowing God.

Initially we begin, therefore, by listening to ourselves at the deepest level and find that, in fact, we are listening to God. We become aware that this deepest level of our being is the voice of God, the Ground of Being, speaking to us. It is what the prophet Elijah heard. Not in the crashing, booming of earthquake, fire, or wind—all of which are symbols of God's presence and spirit. It was only in the inner stirrings of deep inner experience that Elijah met God. Only by listening to himself did he hear the voice of God.

The mystical tradition within the Christian faith has always known this, but in its overreaction to the hierarchical authority of the church, Protestant orthodoxy enthroned the Bible and preaching as the only ways in which God speaks. As a result, the Protestant tradition has all but lost the discipline of listening to the still, small voice within. The Quakers are an exception and speak of this voice within as the "inner light," which provides the individual with internal illumination for seeing what direction the pathway of life needs to take. This guidance, however, is not derived from some blueprint drawn for us by others. It comes only by trusting and responding to those nudges we sense within. We learn what God requires of us by trusting the miracle of our own being.

Very risky business indeed. There are no guarantees in advance that we will not be mistaken. Instead of forgiveness, we must accept the guilt and the despair that go with the risk of trusting our own instincts and being wrong. Lowell Stryker portrays for us the dilemma.

Maturity or self-realization requires that I become aware of the unique, irreplaceable potentialities of my existence as a person and that I accept the responsibility for actualizing them. Self-realization is a painful, gradual process marked by many reversals, defeats, and disappointments. Since what I was meant to be is different from what anyone else was meant to be, no formula, maxim, generalization, or dogma can distinguish for me between the real and the apparently real . . . Life is exposure to contradiction, error, guilt and regret. Its deepest lessons are taught the worst of all possible ways. Man is the only creature with potential, but this potential is found only *in, through,* and *despite* the bumbling, awkwardness of human development. Children become men and women by risking regret, accepting guilt, and learning from failure.[49]

It takes courage to be ourselves. And the courage does not remove the guilt or despair. Courage, rather, affirms the guilt and despair by taking them into our identity. The old piety of selflessness said there was always the option of forgiveness. The new piety of self-affirmation says there is no such copout. Instead, we must accept the responsibility for our lives and affirm as a part of them the guilt and despair that go with living.

Fortunately, both Jesus and God assume we are sinners. They know, even if we do not, that sin is a fact of human existence. The only possible ethical imperative, therefore, is to sin to the glory of God. The alternative is to curl up in some womblike corner and choose not to live at all. Our confessions of sin are not made in order to remove it but rather to affirm our sin courageously before God. If God is to love us at all, it cannot be in spite of our sin as if it were foreign to our true nature and could be overlooked by divine benevolence. No! If God is to love us, it must be as bonafide sinners. This is where the shoe of traditional religion with its emphasis on God's forgiveness begins to pinch.

Weeds Are for Loving Too

When Gerald Ford granted a presidential pardon to Richard Nixon, a good deal of discussion resulted both for and against his action. One of the delayed reactions was voiced by former Attorney General John Mitchell, who realized that when a pardon is granted and accepted, the recipient is legally guilty. As a result, he was concerned that he and the other Watergate defendants would be presumed guilty because of their association with Nixon.

Basic to orthodox religion is the assertion that God is in the business of granting pardons to those of us who fall short of his perfect will for our lives. For nearly nineteen centuries the church's faith has operated on the assumption that the good news consists of God's forgiveness. As a result, worship services normally provide for a period of confession where Christians acknowledge their sin and ask for God's mercy. This, in turn, is followed by an assurance of pardon: the affirmation that God mercifully grants us forgiveness.

It is precisely the goodness of such news, however, that is brought into question by Nixon's response to the presidential pardon. The fact of the matter is that when the pardon was granted, it had little or no effect on his well-being. Gerald Ford may have felt magnanimous in granting the pardon, but Richard Nixon felt guilty and his depression, the reports said, increased.

One of the basic doctrines of traditional religion is that of the atonement. Rooted in the Old Testament sacrificial system, the doctrine holds that God, being holy and perfect, cannot tolerate our sinfulness. Hence we either must not sin—an impossibility if we are to risk living at all—or our sin must be paid for by some sacrifice. It is only when atonement has been made for our sins that pardon can be granted, and we are made acceptable in God's eyes. The New Testament portrays Jesus Christ as the sacrificial lamb who, by his death, procures atonement with God for us. Since most of the early converts to the Christian faith were themselves Jews and had been raised within the tradition of God's atoning love, such a portrayal was to be expected. Christian theological development, therefore, presented Jesus as the Savior who, on behalf of God, sees our sin, is offended by it, and offers himself as a sacrifice for it, thereby obtaining for us God's pardon. It is across our sinful nature that God in Christ writes his "nevertheless" and makes us acceptable to sacred scrutiny. This theology is still commonly found in the hymns and prayers of the church today as this prayer of confession, taken from the *Book of Common Prayer,* indicates.

Almighty and most merciful Father; We have erred, and strayed from thy ways like lost sheep. We have followed too much the devices and desires of our own hearts. We have offended against thy holy laws. We have left undone those things which we ought to have done; and we have done those things which we ought not to have done; And there is no health in us. But thou, Lord, have mercy upon us, miserable offenders. Spare thou those, O God, who confess their faults. Restore thou those who are penitent; According to thy promises declared unto mankind in Christ Jesus our Lord. And grant, O most merciful Father, for his sake; That we may hereafter live a godly, righteous, and sober life, To the glory of thy holy Name. Amen.[50]

The good news in such a theology is that God, so implored, responds out of his mercy and forgiveness by granting us pardon.

The problem with this theology, for me, is that while God may forgive me and call me righteous, he does so *in spite of* who I am. The reality of my being is, I am a sinner. God must accept me in spite of myself, but certainly not because of who I am. My being is, therefore, denied at the very center of my existence. In my totality I stand before God as both good and bad. But in the presence of him who is the ground of all being, part of my being is rejected. God grants me a pardon and thereby calls me righteous, but he and I both know that I am not righteous. I am a sinner. I am a mixture of wheat and tares. God feels righteous in granting the pardon, but I feel forgiven. Consequently, instead of feeling free, I feel guilty. I may stand acquitted before the jury, but before them I feel awkward and depressed for I know I am, in myself, unacceptable in the eyes of the Judge.

It is against this background that the parable of the wheat and tares takes on explosive significance.

The kingdom of heaven may be compared to a man who sowed good seed in his field; but while men were sleeping, his enemy came and sowed weeds among the wheat, and went away. So when the plants came up and bore grain, then the weeds appeared also. And the servants of the householder came and said to him, "Sir, did you not sow good seed in your field? How then has it weeds?" He said to them, "An enemy has done this." The servants said to him, "Then do you want us to go and gather them?" But he said, "No; lest in gathering the weeds you root up the wheat along with them. Let both grow together until the harvest; and at harvest time I will tell the reapers, "Gather the weeds first and bind them in bundles to be burned, but gather the wheat into my barn."" (Matt. 13:24-30)

The parable seems to assume we are ambiguous people—a mixture of good and bad, righteousness and evil. The assumption squares with our observations of reality. A man, for example, who is capable of great love for his wife and family is also the man who is capable of great fits of anger with his employees. The woman who is gentle with her children may nevertheless be very stubborn. The student who is able to make good grades and show a good deal of creativity is also the young person who exhibits an unfortunate selfishness and lack of concern for others.

The Apostle Paul, fully aware of the ambiguity within himself, cried out, "The good that I would do, I do not; and that which I know I ought not to do, is what I end up doing." (Cf. Rom. 7:19.)

Furthermore, the parable not only recognizes our ambiguity, but seems to suggest the evil cannot be taken out of us without destroying our strengths as well. The two must exist side by side for we are one. We are a unity of wheat and tares. There is a little devil in the best of us and a little angel in the worst. The parable of the wheat and tares, therefore, portrays the Savior in a radically different way than has been understood by traditional theology. Rather than one who focuses his concern upon our sinfulness in order to get rid of it or pardon it, thereby making us acceptable, this Savior makes no distinction between wheat and tares and says, "Let them grow together." Rather than calling attention to the tares, the Savior says, "Let them be." Sin is, therefore, not forgiven, nor is it overlooked. It is simply *included* in the human nature which God loves. God recognizes and honors the wholeness of our being, in both its goodness and its badness. He loves us, not in spite of who we are, but because of who we are.

If such an understanding of this parable is granted, there are three implications that follow.

First, to those who are obsessed with removing the tares from their lives, the parable suggests that God loves us with a radical love beyond human comprehension. He places no qualifications upon that love nor upon us as its recipients. He does not love because we are perfect, nor does he love us only when we are good. He loves us in our wholeness and our wholeness includes both the good and the bad, the sinfulness as well as the righteousness. God does not love us in spite of our nature, he loves us because of our nature. What else can be the meaning of Paul's words, "While we were yet sinners Christ died for us"?

God did not wait until the tares had been removed from the world to love us; he loved us while we were yet sinners.

When we look at Jesus, we see God's desire become flesh. That is to say, when we look at Jesus in the company of tax collectors, prostitutes, and sinners, when we see him willing to undergo the suffering and death of the cross, we see God's wish to be with his world—not because he must, in order to expiate sin—but because he prefers the company of the sinners in this world to that of the angels in heaven. The parable suggests that God loves us with an unbelievable and radical love. He values the whole field: wheat and tares. He loves sinners created in his image.

Secondly, the parable speaks of those obsessed with taking out the tares in each others' lives. Probably that includes most of us. We spend a good bit of time trying to reform one another. I have been married to one woman for over twenty-eight years. This morning when I finished shaving, I reached for the towel to dry my face. The towel was gone. It had been thrown in the laundry last night by my good wife. For twenty-eight years she has been gathering the towels and washing them and for twenty-eight years she has never put a towel back. For twenty-eight years she has known that I like to dry my face when I am finished shaving. For twenty-eight years I have tried to reform her to my specifications, and for twenty-eight years she has stubbornly refused to change one iota in this regard.

For twenty-eight years, of course, my wife has had to put up with the residual effects of a conditioned male chauvinism. The parable's assertion, therefore, cuts both ways and raises the question for us: If we can't love each other in our sin, how can we love each other in our goodness? The two are inseparably entwined. I have no reason to assume the next twenty-eight years will be any different from the first, at least with regard to my wife's remembering to put a towel on the towel bar, nor does she expect me to change my chauvinistic peeve. If we cannot love the tares in each other's life, we cannot love the beauty of the wheat either.

I am indebted to my father for many things, but one of the things that I cherish most is something he said to me hours after my mother's death. He said, "Bob, you know last night I saw her bathing in the bath tub, and she was beautiful." My father thought that my seventy-six-year-old mother had a beautiful body. Many of us seem to be obsessed with dieting and exercising *in order* to make ourselves acceptable to our marriage partners. The parable says if we cannot love our spouse in their flabbiness and with rolls of fat, we cannot love them in their trim firmness. We do not love a person now and then, here or there. We love them in their ambiguous wholeness or we do not love them at all.

The parable addresses itself to those who feel the purpose of life is to remove the evil from human nature. It implies that the soil can sustain both wheat and tares without injury to the crop. The parable portrays a landlord who is not interested in the tares. His concern is in helping the wheat to grow. It is the wheat that is of importance. The tares are of little consequence. The accent, therefore, is on the positives of human nature, not the negatives.

One graduate school tells its doctoral candidates that they will pass or fail, not on the basis of what they do not know, but on what they have learned. The purpose of life, as seen by Jesus, is to increase a person's strengths and to enable him or her to grow in size. My two daughters, Christie and Susan, are taking piano lessons. As they progress to increasingly more difficult compositions, they continue to make mistakes and hit sour notes, but the beauty of their music is increasing as well. The aim of piano instruction, I take it, is to enable them to play ever more difficult, complex, and beautiful pieces of music, rather than simply concentrating on removing the mistakes from the ones they can play. Making mistakes is a necessary part of their growing ability to play beautiful music. So with our lives. Making mistakes is a necessary part of our increasing capacity to embrace life's invitations to dance.

Such is the ambiguity of the moral life. The reality in which a person's spirit is expressed is a mixture of good and bad. How far the person has come and how large he or she is can only be appreciated when we see the difficulties and the conflicts, both within and without, with which they have had to wrestle. The Scottish poet Robert Burns was an alcoholic and a dirty old man by the standards of many. Yet what magnificent poetry he wrote, and what a magnificent grasp of life he had! His understanding of the human dilemma with its visions of grace was possible only because of his own internal battles and struggles. To have taken out the tares in his life would have destroyed the wheat as well.

As we grow in size, we do not diminish the ambiguity. To grow in size is to be increasingly amazed at the mystery within. The tares will always be with us. So while religion discusses what to do with them in terms of guilt and pardons, Jesus addresses us with a reminder that weeds are for loving too. It is important for us to hear him because without such a word of Grace and the permission it gives to risk making mistakes, we might sit out the dance of life. The chaperone of conscience will see to it.

Counteracting Conscience

"Conscience doth make cowards of us all," said Shakespeare. It was a problem for Hamlet. It is a problem for us all. When it comes to the risk of being who we are, conscience doth indeed make cowards of us all. By the time we have celebrated our fortieth birthday, not only has the child in us been deeply buried, but we have developed a burly conscience to guard against the escape of the fool and the lover from their subterranean prison in the unconscious. Yet the Bible keeps prodding us, calling us to risk living and loving.

My children, love must not be a matter of words or talk; it must be genuine, and show itself in action. This is how we may know that we belong to the realm of truth, and convince ourselves in his sight that even if our conscience condemns us, God is greater than our conscience and knows all.

Dear friends, if our conscience does not condemn us, then we can approach God with confidence, and obtain from him whatever we ask, because we are keeping his commands and doing what he approves. This is his command: to give our allegiance to his Son Jesus Christ and love one another as he commanded. (1 John 3:18-23, The New English Bible)

The assertion of John is clear: We are commanded to love one another. His message is not apt to make front-page news headlines, however. It is like advocating apple pie, baseball, and a sound dollar.

But there is something strange about John's message. He is talking about justifying such a trite invitation to love in the face of a disturbed conscience. Upon closer examination, we see he is talking about something morally risky. He is not only calling us to love in deed and in truth—that is to say, to put our action where our mouth is—he is also saying that if we do so, we could well be embarking upon dangerous waters. Loving is risky business.

Take, for example, the issue of human rights in some Third World countries. Despite our nation's outcry against the physical abuse of political protesters in El Salvador, the beatings, torture, and murder by the military death squads continue. Few official voices have been raised in objection, and Salvadoran church leaders as well as citizens who speak out against the brutality literally risk life and limb. They are called "communists" and disappear, some never to be heard from again. Others are found brutally murdered.

Love of humanity is risky business in certain parts of the world. Examples, of course, abound closer to home, but it is always easier to make the point by looking at the speck in our neighbor's eye than examining the logjam in our own. The point, nonetheless, is to do as John says and put our action where our mouth is. This often invites repercussions of the most serious sort.

But John is not only talking about loving that is physically dangerous, he is referring to something that is morally dangerous as well. If we love one another, we are inviting feelings that can be threatening. I frequently conduct human awareness workshops in which participants get in touch with some of their inner feelings and have an opportunity to share them with others. Out of such sharing comes the bonding of human friendship. One of the activities is a touching exercise. Almost without exception, when men touch men, or participants touch someone other than their own spouses, feelings of anxiety arise. Their feelings are born of what Tillich calls "the anxiety of the possible." We are made vaguely aware of emotions that *could* be. We sense feelings that might develop and of which society disapproves.

Yet this is precisely what we are invited to risk by John's admonition to love one another. We are not to hold life at arm's length nor to keep others at what might be a safe distance from us. As Keen once remarked, "To play it cool in life is to risk becoming frigid." To be a Christian is to be called to risk precisely these feelings and emotions that we sense as threatening and upon which society frowns.

Howard Thurman consequently concludes:

If all this is true, then it is clear that any structure of society, any arrangement under which human beings live, that does not provide maximum opportunities for free-flowing circulation among one another, works against social and individual health. Any attitudes, private or group, which prohibit people from coming into "across-the-board" contact with each other work against the implementation of the love ethic. So considered, segregation, prescriptions of separation, are a disease of the human spirit and the body politic. It does not matter how meaningful the tight circle of isolated security may be, in which individuals or groups move. The very existence of such circles, whether regarded as a necessity of religious faith, political ideology, or social purity, precludes the possibility of the experience of love as a part of the necessity of man's life.[51]

Right away conscience is there to tell us this is dangerous talk. What about national security? What about the sanctity of marriage and the unity of the family? It is, in fact, the business of conscience to tell us to do right and avoid the wrong. It reminds us we are always to think properly and act morally. The vocabulary of conscience is laced with multitudes of "shoulds" and "oughts." As a result, conscience can be an authoritarian preacher demanding of us conduct which is correct because it is morally safe and secure.

Deitrich Bonhoeffer offers a classic description of the religious person whose life is centered around being good and whose conduct is governed by an articulate conscience. He speaks of such a person—the Pharisee—as,

that extremely admirable man who subordinates his entire life to his knowledge of good and evil and is as severe a judge of himself as of his neighbour to the honour of God, whom he humbly thanks for this knowledge. For the Pharisee every moment of life becomes a situation of conflict in which he has to choose between good and evil . . . . The Pharisee is not opinionated; special situations and emergencies receive special consideration; forbearance and generosity are not excluded by the gravity of the knowledge of good and evil; they are rather an expression of this gravity. And there is no rash presumption here, or arrogance or unverified self-esteem. The Pharisee is fully conscious of his own faults and of his duty of humility and thankfulness towards God. But, of course, there are differences, which for God's sake must not be disregarded, between the sinner and the man who strives towards good, between the man who becomes a breaker of the law out of a situation of wickedness and the man who does so out of necessity. If anyone disregards these differences, if he fails to take every factor into account in each of the innumerable cases of conflict, he sins against the knowledge of good and evil.[52]

Clearly the Pharisee is not a bad guy lurking behind a handlebar mustache. But the Pharisee is so focused on being good that he misses seeing the scenery and the natives along the way. His problem is he has an overdeveloped conscience and has trouble getting close to people.

When a group of Pharisees observed Jesus' healing a man on the Sabbath, they objected because the healing offended their sense of morality. The Law must be kept at all costs, even at the expense of a diseased person for whom love could be shown. Similarly, Jesus committed, in their eyes, the almost unforgivable sin by eating and drinking with sinners. For the Pharisee it was far better to disassociate one's self from human beings than to be contaminated by their humanity.

Religious people, and especially those of us strongly identified with institutional religion, tend to suffer from overdeveloped consciences. Like muscle-bound weight lifters who lose body agility and cannot move quickly, we as religious people often become conscience-bound and lose the ability to love. We can become so fearful of moral contamination that we are unable to risk involving ourselves in life. To become the servant of the tyrant, conscience, is to draw the circle of life ever tighter around us in a safe and secure cocoon that, nevertheless, insulates us from the vast arena where life is being lived.

How is it we become enslaved to conscience? Why is it we listen to this vendor of "shoulds" and "oughts"? Why is it we so willingly carry the heavy yoke of religion on our shoulders? It is because we as human beings are aware of death. And because we are aware of specific death, we try to insure against it. We go to the doctor once a year for a checkup. We take vitamins. We exercise a lot. We look both ways before we cross the street.

W. C. Fields, who was certainly not—by any usual definition of the term—a religious man, was discovered reading a Bible during the final days of his life. When asked what he was doing, he replied with dry humor that he was looking for loopholes. In middle age we look for loopholes. We take out insurance policies, not only on our life here, but on the life hereafter. We like to ensure against the odds on eternity by obeying the "shoulds" and "oughts" so we may be sure of heavenly reward. These moral "musts," which our insecurity lays on us, ensuring us against vulnerability and keeping us safe and secure, constitute the religious impulse that produces those inner preachers who tell us what we must do or ought to be.

Middle age is a time when we become acutely aware of our vulnerability and approaching death. It is a time of crisis. We can choose to sell our birthright for a mess of pottage—that is, sell our souls to the secure bondage of conscience—or risk dancing with the God of Grace. To all who are tyrannized by the heavy burden of an overactive conscience Jesus says, "Come to me, all who labor and are heavy laden, and I will give you rest. Take my yoke upon you, and learn from me; . . . For my yoke is easy, and my burden is light" (Matt. 11:28-30).

Tillich comments on this demand laid on us by Jesus:

Nothing is demanded of you—no idea of God, and no goodness in yourselves, not your being religious, not your being Christian, not your being wise, and not your being moral. But what is demanded is only your being open and willing to accept what is given to you, the New Being, the being of love and justice and truth, as it is manifest in Him Whose yoke is easy and Whose burden is light.[53]

Jesus is not the founder of some new religion; he is the conqueror of all religion. When Jesus says, "Take up your cross and follow me," he is not laying some new religious demand on us upon which conscience can feed like a parasite. It is not a new obligation that we *should* undertake. Rather, the cross is the realization that God has said *no* to all of our religious attempts to catch his attention. They offer no refuge for us. We cannot hide from the frightening realization that we alone must bear responsibility for our lives.

From a historical perspective, the crucifixion of Jesus was perpetrated by religious leaders with the highest aspirations and impeccable moral character. But it was their religious achievements that failed to lift the scales from their eyes so they could see Jesus for who he was! A religious conscience is no guide to the Truth. Religious people guided by good conscience failed to see in Jesus the Word of Divine Wisdom. He was crucified by religious people. God has shown us in the cross that the way of conscience will not save us.

Therefore, John reminds us that God does not command us to obey our conscience. Conscience is socially derived. It is programmed by cultural mores. We are conditioned to do right and avoid wrong as defined by cultural standards. But anthropologists point out that what is wrong in one culture may be right in another. There is no universally held right and wrong. Conscience always tells us to do what is right, but it never informs us what the right is. The point being: There is nothing particularly Christian about having a conscience, much less obeying it.

What God does require, John says, is to believe in Jesus Christ and love one another. Apparently there is something about believing in him that frees us from the tyranny of conscience so that we can risk loving one another. The question is: What does it mean, functionally, to believe in Christ?

I submit that to believe in Jesus Christ means to believe nothing can ever hurt us spiritually. "Sin" and "sinner" are words that, for us, no longer have significance. In the crucifixion and resurrection of Christ, we are given permission to rename our lives, including the errors that inevitably result from risking to live them fully. The resurrection gives us permission to rename our lives and our experiences *gracefully*. It does so by introducing an element of humor into the deadly serious game of living.

Humor is that graceful view of life that refuses to take a given situation seriously. It does not look at things as they are and, therefore, will not allow the facts to define the reality. Humor looks at the predicament from a different perspective and sees another kind of reality: the reality of Grace. By refusing to recognize the situation as Lord, it transcends the tragedy. Sometimes people who are frightened joke. The humor frees them from the incapacitating power of fear. When people who are nervous laugh, the humor neutralizes the embarrassing power of self-consciousness.

Similarly, Jesus Christ is God's sense of humor made flesh. In his Resurrection God's sense of humor refuses to take our human limitations seriously. The Resurrection is God's Gracefull sense of humor that frees us to laugh at the destructive power of sin and death. Their stranglehold on us is, thereby, broken. Death and all its symbols are seen from a different perspective.

A cartoon depicts two hapless fellows chained hand and foot, suspended by ropes over a pit filled with crocodiles. Sharpened swords protrude from the sides of the pit. The situation is quite hopeless. But one fellow says to the other, "Now here's my plan."

Into the human predicament, with all of its apparent hopelessness, God throws his punch line. Suddenly, all human limitations: neurotic jealousy and anger, self-consciousness and incapacitating pride, suffering and death; all are viewed from a different perspective. To us, caught in the hopelessness of the predicament, God tells his joke; the Word becomes flesh in Jesus Christ. As Jesus hangs helplessly on his cross, God says, "Now here's my plan." And the plan is Resurrection.

Death and despair are trumped by God. He has the last laugh. The Resurrection is God's sense of humor. Because of it human weaknesses and limitations are seen not to be the defining characteristic of our humanity. Our failings neither limit nor define us. In it we see things, not as they apparently are, but as they can be by God's Grace. We can live with hope. We can live gracefully. As a result, to believe in Jesus Christ, to believe in his life, death, and Resurrection, is to see we have been given permission by God to live in the full knowledge that nothing can ever spiritually hurt us nor destroy us, not even sin or death. As Paul puts it, "We are afflicted in every way, but not crushed; perplexed, but not driven to despair; . . . struck down, but not destroyed" (2 Cor. 4:8,9).

The resurrection of Jesus makes it clear sin cannot hold us; and, therefore, we can risk living, and we can risk sinning. When we recognize that to live is to sin, we relax and sin to the glory of God. You would not say that to just anybody, but you would say it to followers of Christ who are seriously trying to follow the command to love one another. For only as we are given permission to sin to the glory of God can we risk living and loving to the glory of God.

We can, of course, find many reasons for doing neither. And it goes without saying that they are good reasons, for we would never be caught dead with mere excuses. Perhaps it is more accurate to say it is the only way we will be caught with our excuses for not living now. Nevertheless, one of the most respectable-sounding reasons for putting off living is that we have to keep one eye on our heavenly reward and the other on our present responsibilities.

Living Now

When Robin Roberts received one of the many awards in his long and colorful baseball career, he received it with proper modesty and words to the effect that his real ambition was to get to heaven where the great award would be given. His humble acceptance speech illustrates a widespread assumption held by many of us: The purpose of life is to get to heaven.

Heaven is where the action is. Everything else is secondary and preliminary. What we do here in this world, with this life, is only of significance in light of its meaning for the otherworld, beyond death. The kingdom of God is understood as other-worldly and is even called by some the kingdom of heaven. Matthew, for example, characteristically refers to it in this manner. What happens here in this world pales into insignificance in light of the greater value of the next. This life is of no great concern because it is the next life that matters. The action is not here, not now, but yet to come, in the future, in the kingdom of heaven.

It is further assumed that the kingdom of heaven is a desirable place and anyone with any sense will want to get in. The alternative to life in the Kingdom is unattractive at best.

In light of these assumptions, it is revealing to look at Jesus' parable about God's kingdom and those who enter it.

When one of those who sat at table with [Jesus] heard this, he said to him, "Blessed is he who shall eat bread in the kingdom of God!" But [Jesus] said to him, "A man once gave a great banquet, and invited many; and at the time for the banquet he sent his servant to say to those who had been invited, 'Come; for all is now ready.' But they all alike began to make excuses. The first said to him, 'I have bought a field, and I must go out and see it; I pray you, have me excused.' And another said, 'I have bought five yoke of oxen, and I go to examine them; I pray you, have me excused.' And another said, 'I have married a wife, and therefore I cannot come.'" (Luke 14:15-20)

In the parable Jesus reflects on our reluctance to attend the banquet of the Kingdom. Initially, it appears as though he is, in fact, talking about the kingdom of heaven—that is to say, life after death. As one of Jesus' listeners remarked, the food must be marvelous and the service great, "Blessed is he who shall eat bread in the kingdom of God."

What is interesting, however, is Jesus' response. It is introduced with the word "but." It is clear Jesus has no intention of confirming our assumptions, much less elaborating on them. Instead, with the word "but," he changes our understanding of the entire matter. He tells a parable about the kingdom banquet prepared by God *but* which is now ready. Dinner is *now* being served. Not in the future. *Now!*

The word "now" refers to that moment of time that is continually moving but in which all living takes place. We may have memories of the past, we may have hopes for the future, but it is in the *now* that living occurs. Clearly, therefore, the banquet of the kingdom of God is not life after death. It has nothing to do with heaven. It has to do with life right here and now. The art of kingdom living is learning to live in the *now*.

It is characteristic of youth to look forward to the "day when . . . ." and often senility is obsessed with recalling the past. The in-between years offer an increasing awareness of the importance of the present, providing us with both the experience of the past and an urgency and desire to live future days, which are numbered. The parable, therefore, has special relevance for the middle years and calls us to live *now* in the kingdom of the God of Grace.

But each one to whom the invitation was given began to make excuses. Sound familiar? The concerns of the middle years press in upon us. We have responsibilities and obligations. One of the invited guests said, "I have just purchased a yoke of oxen. Please have me excused. I must go and examine them." Quite clearly in his value system the oxen were more important than the banquet. The labels that we paste over life prioritize our values and predispose us to experience one thing and block out another. As a result, the banquet is not as important as the technology of production. The *now* of eating the banquet is missed in favor of the *now* of examining the oxen. To choose one thing is to exclude another, and our choices are often determined by our labeling of what is important.

The point can be illustrated by noting an interesting difference in the goals of two forms of oriental meditation. The purpose of ZaZen Buddhist meditation is not to wipe the mind clean or keep it blank, as is the intent of Transcendental Meditation in Hindu practice, but rather to expand the mind so it can take in *all* the experiences of the moment. We are experiencing a great deal of life right now but are probably not aware of it. Stop for just a minute and focus on your stomach. Be aware of how it feels right now. Is it hungry or full, knotted or relaxed? How do you experience your little finger this instant? Something we take for granted is our breathing. Listen for a moment and be aware of each inhalation and exhalation. Right this moment a lot of living is occurring, but we miss much of it because we have labelled it "unimportant," or "trivial."

When we see dandelions growing in our lawn, we call them "undesirable," but dandelions are just as much a miracle of nature, and every bit as beautiful, as grass. It is just that our society has labeled them "weeds"; and, therefore, we do not appreciate them.

So it was with the man invited to eat at the banquet. He said, "I have something more important to do." He missed the *now* of living in the kingdom of God, just as he probably missed the miracle of a sunset because at the moment it was "intruding" into his work, or the softness of a child's touch because at the time it was an "interruption," or the wisdom in a chance comment because right then it was "irrelevant." He missed the banquet of life. The labels with which he tagged the data of the moment blinded him to the graceful surprises of the Kingdom.

Another person missed the banquet because he was a man of means. He had invested in property. It was his hope that the future would bring an increase of value to his investment and he would make some money in real estate. He was borrowing on the future. It was the next moment, not *now,* that held the promise to be claimed. So he postponed living in the *now* because he was banking on tomorrow.

Tomorrow we will take time for ourselves. Tomorrow we will make plans to begin living. Tomorrow we will enjoy the scenery along the way. In the parable Jesus reminds us the art of kingdom living is to live *now.* There may not be any tomorrows.

Earlier I spoke of the Buddhist monk who, though faced with certain death, nevertheless took time to pluck and eat the strawberry growing on a ledge. Embodied in the story is the secret of kingdom living: living in the *now*. Many of us would have said in such a situation, "I can't eat that strawberry. I have to find a way out of this predicament." But there was no way out. We would like to have a future, but there are no guarantees we will have one. We ought to have a tomorrow, but we may not. We have today. We have this moment, and that is all of which we can be sure. Bounded by death, and with the mouse already gnawing at the vine to which we cling, we may call death obscene, but it does not change its reality. Sören Kierkegaard observed that the earnest thought of death is life's greatest ally. It is the full realization of the tigers above and below, and the clock running, that causes us to treasure the strawberries of life.

The hospice movement speaks of terminally ill patients living with cancer rather than dying from it. The invitation is there to live a rich, full life, even in the last moments; a life enriched by the acceptance of death's inevitability and of life's beauty and meaning. The art of living in the kingdom of God is learning how to live in the *now* and to eat the strawberries because, if we do not eat them now, we will never taste them.

The third person who made an excuse for not attending the banquet is the most intriguing of all. Why did Jesus put him in the story? In the moment of invitation to live in the kingdom of God *now,* to eat at the banquet *now,* this man remembered his obligations. He was a responsible married man. He had to go home to his wife. He had taken vows to love, honor, and be true to her "until death do us part." He was, in every sense, an honorable man. And Jesus said he, too, missed the banquet!

Whence cometh this voice that, at the moment of invitation to live *now,* reminds us of our responsibilities to the past and our obligations to the future. It is that voice of conscience, spoken of earlier, and its job is to keep us in line by reminding us of the Law: that myriad of customs and taboos, values and morals, that—when violated—makes us feel guilty and, thereby, keeps us true to our obligations and responsibilities.

Jesus summarized the Law with the admonition to love God, our neighbor, and ourselves. It seems simple enough, but loving gets complicated by past responsibility and future obligations. Take, for example, his clarification of this point in the parable of the Good Samaritan (Luke 10:29-37). There was the priest who saw this poor soul in the ditch but hurried by because he had a responsibility to get to church on time. He had to preach a sermon or administer the sacrament to the waiting troops. A good clergyperson, a fine preacher, a respected member of the ecclesiastical hierarchy, but he missed the banquet, says Jesus.

And then along came the Levite, who also saw the problem. But he passed by on the other side because he had things to do, places to go, and people to see. He had a reputation to uphold. By middle age a person has invested a lot of time and energy in building a reputation. He had to think of his good name in the community. He was not about to turn aside from such obligations to help this poor soul. It might have been a damsel in distress and, had he been required to take her to an inn, that is, to a motel, and take care of her, that would be much too risky for his good name. What would people think?

We might add: It could have been an American citizen, true-blue and loyal, who passed by when it was learned the poor fellow was a Communist sympathizer. Or a married woman who felt obliged to pass by on the other side because to share the company of another man is a "no-no." It might have been an athlete from our alma mater, who passed by on the other side because school spirit demands that we *not* appreciate the marvelous catch by an opposing player, which defeated the home team. So, one by one, we pass by on the other side because there are obligations to which we must be loyal, responsibilities to which we must be true, traditions and principles that must be upheld.

But then came the Samaritan. And he responded to the invitation of the moment. He loved his neighbor. From the point of view of the Law, the Samaritan was a heretic, a blasphemer, immoral. No doubt a child molester and a homosexual. Jews had no dealings with Samaritans. But all those labels are applicable only if one is obligated to Jewish Law. The razor edge of Jesus' parable cut the Gordian knot and opened up the corridors of new possibilities. This man was a Samaritan. He was not obligated to Jewish Law. The Law was relative. He was free of it. So he turned aside to love *now.*

The superior man, said Confucius, goes through life without a preconceived course of action or any taboos. He merely decides in the moment what is the right thing to do. From a traditional point of view, such a precept is usually regarded as a recommendation of caprice, or an invitation to disorder. We feel that, unless the Law is held over our heads like a club, reminding us of our obligations to the past and our responsibilities to the future, we shall revert to our basic and natural depravity. God's will is understood as something foreign to us and alien to our inclinations; something to which we must bend our will in self-negation. In point of fact, the New Testament agrees with Confucius. Paul reminds us, "For freedom Christ has set us free; stand fast therefore, and do not submit again to a yoke of slavery" (Gal. 5:1).

Paul, of course, was talking about the yoke of the Law, because it can keep us from feasting at the banquet in the kingdom of God *now*. To be free in Christ is not the same thing as doing our own thing It is to be free for the other. But to be free in Christ is both radical and risky. It means not being hampered by past or future connections that prevent us from responding to life's invitation to be at the banquet *now*. We are free to be fully present and available to the other—any other—in the present moment.

What seemed, at first, to be the most honorable of all reasons for not attending the banquet is, in the final analysis, just as problematic as the rest.

Life is for living, and the parable comes as an invitation with our address on it.

The clock is running. The seconds are ticking away. Yet, by the grace of God we have been given—right now—another breath to draw, another chance to dance. He has prepared a great banquet and invited many. He has sent his servant to say to those who have ears to hear, "Come, for all is *now* ready."

The R.S.V.P. is ours to write.

Conclusion

Risking the Miracle

By reading the Bible from the vantage point of middle age we have become less impressed with its authority and more amazed at its wisdom. Reading it through bifocals has enabled us to see the relativity of religious authority and the gracefulness of life. Its stories and faith statements have provided us with a perspective from which to understand our experience as people of faith.

The turbulence of the mid-life crisis brings with it the invitation to dance with the God of grace. We are ready to risk the dance because there is a certain self-confidence that comes with age. We have paid our dues. There are some things we know. If our society has not yet come to value the crisis of mid-life and the new possibilities that it brings, that is society's problem. I, at least, do not want to be deprived of the benefits of my age. I have earned them. In our youth-oriented culture there is something pathetic about trying to pretend we do not grow older. There is no great virtue in being thirty-nine and holding. Maturity is an asset. May Sarton examines this asset with regard to love.

It looks as if T. S. Eliot came into a fully consummated happy marriage only when he was seventy. Yeats married when he was fifty or over. I am coming into the most fulfilled love of my life now. But for some reason Americans are terrified of the very idea of passionate love going on past middle age. Are they afraid of being alive? Do they want to be dead, i.e., *safe?* For of course one is never safe when in love. Growth is demanding and may seem dangerous, for there is loss as well as gain in growth. But why go on living if one has ceased to grow? And what more demanding atmosphere for growth than love in any form, than any relationship which can call out and requires of us our most secret and deepest selves?

My neighbor who wishes to remain thirty-nine indefinitely does so out of anxiety—she is afraid she will no longer be "attractive" if people know her age. But if one wants mature relationships, one will look for them among one's peers. I cannot imagine being in love with someone much younger than I because I have looked on love as an *education sentimentale*. About love I have little to learn from the young.[54]

Mid-life can be exhilarating. There is a certain magic to middle age. We have used the term "miracle" to describe it. But the real miracle is the gift of life itself, and when we look at the miracle become flesh in Christ we are better able to appreciate it in ourselves.

Unfortunately, there is no story in the Christmas collection that is better known and less understood than Luke's story concerning the miracle of Jesus' birth. It has become clouded with seasonal sentimentality or calcified in dogmatic literalism. Yet perhaps it can speak to us as we conclude our discussion of mid-life and its possibilities.

In the sixth month the angel Gabriel was sent from God to a city of Galilee named Nazareth, to a virgin betrothed to a man whose name was Joseph, of the house of David; and the virgin's name was Mary . . . . And the angel said to her, "Do not be afraid, Mary, for you have found favor with God. And behold, you will conceive in your womb and bear a son, and you shall call his name Jesus . . . ." And Mary said to the angel, "How shall this be, since I have no husband?" And the angel said to her, "The Holy Spirit will come upon you, and the power of the Most High will overshadow you; therefore the child to be born will be called holy, the Son of God." (Luke 1:26-35)

Sadly, many Christians have made the virgin birth an article of faith. Unless we believe in it, along with a belief in the literal physical resurrection of Jesus, we do not qualify for the team. It is unfortunate not only because a literal understanding of the story requires suspension of our rational mind, substituting instead belief in a "miracle," but more importantly, because it misunderstands the nature of the story itself.

Luke's account was not written to make a biological assertion about Jesus. His concern was not to tell us how the conception of Jesus took place. Consequently, taking the story literally gets us nowhere. Even if we grant—for the sake of argument—that Luke was telling us a historical fact, what do we have? We have a baby conceived in a woman's womb without benefit of male sperm. But note! That does not make the child the Son of God. It merely makes him a medical freak. To be born of a virgin no more makes Jesus the Son of God than it would if he had been born with three heads. It simply makes him a biological curiosity. Even if we take the story literally, therefore, we still have to make the leap of faith about who Jesus was and is.

But, returning to the story: Luke did not tell it to make a biological assertion about the origin of Jesus. Rather, he wanted to make a *theological* statement. Luke calls us to see the impossibility of this man's humanity. He is human in a way in which we are not human. We cannot account for this man's humanity by adding up male sperm and female egg: Joseph plus Mary. Normal origins cannot account for this amazing person. So the story was written to point up the miraculous humanity of Jesus, using the idiom of the day: a story of virgin birth. The Greco-Roman world in which Luke wrote was full of saviors. If Luke was going to get a hearing for his savior, he had to at least present the credentials that all of the competing saviors claimed; namely, to be born of the gods.

The relevance of the story for us, however, is its invitation to consider on the one hand the miracle of Jesus' humanity and, on the other, the miracle of our own. I use the term "invitation" advisedly because the story does not push us, it does not demand of us, it only nudges us in the direction of amazement. It invites us to look at our own birth—not the how of it but the fact that it took place at all. It is this sense of uniqueness that, when grasped by our imagination, causes us to see the unrepeatable opportunity each of us has to live our life, to experience all of the ups and downs, the joys and the sorrows, which constitute our special adventure. We become aware of the privilege of living—the whole of it, the good as well as the bad.

In a "Peanuts" cartoon Lucy talks to the dog Snoopy: "You know there are times when you really bug me." And then she thinks, "But I also admit there are times when I feel like giving you a hug." So she hugs Snoopy. He stands there with that infectious grin on his face and says, "That's the way I am, buggable and huggable."

Life, like Snoopy, is buggable and huggable, but we get attached to it. Considering the alternative, it is nice to have around. We instinctively resent not living. We resent our death. By middle age we have tasted enough to know we want the whole loaf. We see life as too short to meet all of the people, experience all of the pleasures, love all the lovable people, visit all of the world's cultures, see all of the waterfalls and sunsets. It is too short to do it all, and that is why it is such a gift to be able to do any of it.

The account, then, that Luke gives us is a story of amazing life, and it not only invites us to see our lives as miracles but to risk living them as such. The question is, how do we risk living a miracle?

It is generally assumed that miracles are God's business. It goes with the job description. A miracle is something that God alone can do. A mighty act that only she can accomplish. Something amazing happens and it is attributed to God's intervention. Dead people are brought back to life. Deaf people are made to hear. The lame walk and dance. The sea is calmed and water becomes a surface upon which Jesus and Peter can walk. Food is multiplied to feed the waiting crowd, and water is turned into wine.

But, why is it, then, that in all of these Bible stories *Jesus,* not God, is the one credited with the miracle? Turning water into wine, for example? That the water became wine—that the molecules were altered in such a way as to transform water chemically into wine—is obviously the Creator's doing, not Jesus'. Why, then, is Jesus credited with the miracle?

If we dispose of the matter by saying Jesus was God, or the Son of God, what we have done is rendered this story, and the others like it, irrelevant, a curiosity gathering dust in a museum. If Jesus is *merely* divine, then of course he can turn water into wine. What else would you expect of Divinity? But the story, unfortunately, has absolutely no relevance for living our lives, for we are not gods.

I am not for a minute suggesting that Jesus performed no miracles. Quite the contrary. He did. Many, in fact. But they were the kind of miracles that *all of us* can perform. And therein lies their relevance for us. Anyone can risk a miracle.

A similar point is made in Richard Bach's book *Illusions.* Bach raises the provocative question "What would it mean if Jesus were to come back into our time?" The plot of the story, therefore, deals with a young pilot named Richard who encounters a kind of messiah figure known as Donald Shimoda, also a pilot. They are sitting in a pasture after a day of barnstorming in their planes. Richard, who is learning about life and the messianic possibilities of everyone, notices Shimoda playing the guitar.

"Donald, that's beautiful! I didn't know you could play the guitar!"

"You didn't? Then you think somebody could have walked up to Jesus the Christ and handed him a guitar and he would have said, 'I can't play that thing.' Would he have said that?"

Shimoda put the guitar back in its place and walked out into the sunlight with me. "Or if somebody came by who spoke Russian or Persian, do you think any master worth his aura would not know what he was saying? Or if he wanted to skin a D-10 Cat or fly an airplane, that he couldn't do it?"

"So you really know all things, don't you?"

"You do too, of course. I just know that I know all things."

"I could play the guitar like that?"

"No, you'd have your own style, different from mine."

"How do I do that?" I wasn't going to run back and buy the guitar, I was just curious.

"Just give up all your inhibitions and all your beliefs that you can't play. Touch the thing as though it was a part of your life, which it is, in some alternate lifetime. Know that it's all right for you to play it well, and let your nonconscious self take over your fingers and play."[55]

The problem with Bach's concept is that he locates the miracle in *playing* the guitar rather than in *picking it up.* The miracle is our *willingness to risk* playing the guitar. It is divine capability to be able to do all things. But by middle age we are under no illusions about our divine possibilities. For us as mortals the miracle rests in our willingness to dare thinking beyond the accustomed limits. It is risking belief that with God all things are possible.

The Gospel writer, John, sees this distinction and tells a more realistic, and therefore, more helpful story about Jesus.

On the third day there was a marriage at Cana in Galilee, and the mother of Jesus was there; Jesus also was invited to the marriage, with his disciples. When the wine gave out, the mother of Jesus said to him, "They have no wine." And Jesus said to her, "O woman, what have you to do with me? My hour has not yet come." His mother said to the servants, "Do whatever he tells you." Now six stone jars were standing there, for the Jewish rites of purification, each holding twenty or thirty gallons. Jesus said to them, "Fill the jars with water." And they filled them up to the brim. He said to them, "Now draw some out, and take it to the steward of the feast." So they took it. When the steward of the feast tasted the water now become wine, and did not know where it came from (though the servants who had drawn the water knew), the steward of the feast called the bridegroom and said to him, "Every man serves the good wine first; and when men have drunk freely, then the poor wine; but you have kept the good wine until now." (John 2:1-10)

Do you see the miracle? Jesus risked serving water to the steward of the feast *believing that it could become wine.* Water into wine? "Impossible!" we would say. But that is the miracle: *Jesus did not think it was impossible.* If God had failed to turn the molecules of water into wine, that would not have diminished Jesus' miracle one iota. For Jesus the miracle was daring to believe all things are possible. If we have faith as a mustard seed, he promised, nothing shall be impossible. He was saying if we dare to risk a miracle, nothing can own us, nothing can restrict us, nothing can define us! Whether or not God comes through is not the issue. The point of risking a miracle is that we are not confined. If God does not see the exciting possibilities of our risk, that is her problem, not ours. Our miracle is daring to risk being outrageously creative with our lives.

"I'm not concerned with ideas which are merely true," Alfred North Whitehead once said, "Come to me with ideas which are interesting." Jesus might well say something similar to us. "Don't come to me with lives which are merely good. Come with lives that are interesting."

We can sense the frustration in Jesus when he looked out over the crowd and exclaimed, "O faithless and perverse generation, how long am I to bear with you?" (Matt. 17:17). Living with dull, shortsighted, safe people must have been a drag for such an impossibly creative person.

Some years ago, while working with a group of senior high young people, I asked them to express poetically their understanding of life. One of the group contributed these words:

> Why do you sit there silent.
> For sanity sake, can't you say anything?
> Something real,
> Anything before I drown in a sea of nursery rhymes.
> Not a tin hallelujah that will rust and sink—
> Something that will live.
> Something like a dream.

Risking a miracle is daring to dream. But the problem is that adult society has little use for dreams or dreamers.

Like the characters in Beckett's play *Waiting for Godot,* most of us script life as a matter of sitting around waiting for something to happen. We assume the die is cast. We are resigned to our fate. We wait for God to intervene with the miracles. Of course, there are times when we have to wait, for we have no alternative. But the one thing we do not ever have to wait for is the *opportunity* to live. That opportunity is here *now.* And by virtue of that fact, we are invited to make our lives a miracle. To do so is to live them *fully* . . . savoring each and every experience in our threescore and ten years, enjoying the multitude of possibilities, saying *yes* to life.

God calls us to be great lovers—not only in bed, but great lovers of life. We are called to live life passionately. It is instructive that Jesus' last days are called "Passion Week." Why? Because he lived them so fully, even recklessly, that it cost him his life. When Janis Joplin, the famous rock singer died in 1970, hundreds of thousands of people mourned her death. Again, why? *Time* magazine commented,

> Those who knew Janis Joplin only from her records can be forgiven for wondering quite what the fuss was about. It could not be communicated fully on records—the burning lava flow of energy raising audiences to their feet and into the aisles . . . .
> When she threw back her head to sing, she became a lioness. From the moment she stomped, wailed, moaned, sweated her way through *Love is Like a Ball and Chain* at the Monterey pop festival in June 1967 until her death three years later from an overdose of heroin, Janis Joplin was the high priestess of rock.[56]

There was something contagious about her passion for life. And I suspect that passion for life was what was so contagious about Jesus. He dared to live the possibilities. In any case, his life was labeled "passionate." To live passionately as Jesus did is to throw ourselves into life without rationally measuring the cost or calculating all of the consequences. It is daring to live fully every opportunity. It is this love of life that Whitehead calls "A zest for existence" or Tielhard calls "an appetite for being."

But wherever there is that kind of living, that passionate love of life, there is always risk.

It is a risk, of course, because there is no blueprint for my life or yours. My life has never been lived before, nor has yours. It cannot be compared to anyone else's life. It is unique. It is a once-in-a-universe possibility. There are no specifications for it.

But it is also a risk because even when we have apparently gotten our act together and settled on a lifestyle, the terms and conditions of life keep changing. Nothing is ever nailed down finally or settled. The possibilities shift. These changes comprise the identity crises we encounter and constitute the fractures between the various stages in our growth.

German theologian Jurgen Moltmann, in noting these crises concludes,

No lifestyle is valid for all times and all generations. Every lifestyle has its own time and its own term. Every life crisis is always also a crisis of lifestyle. During such crises we note that our modes of life up to this point in time can no longer assimilate and express the new experiences which we are having.[57]

The point to be grasped is that the new experiences we are having each day mean seeing new possibilities on the horizon. Risking a miracle means risking actualizing those possibilities. It means creating something that has never been before. Middle age offers a unique combination of wisdom and perspective to risk such creativity with our lives.

So, it was that a middle-aged Jesus and his mother had an invitation to a wedding. One among many. When they arrived, they discovered the party was in danger of sagging because the wine had run out. Jesus' mother said to him, "Can't you do something about this?" But Jesus replied, "What can I possibly do? We have no money and the stores are closed. It's impos . . . ." And then for the first time, according to John, Jesus risked a new possibility. He said, "Fill the jars with water." And they filled them up to the brim and Jesus said, "Now draw some of the water out and take it to the steward of the feast." So they took it. And the steward tasted it . . . .

This kind of risking calls for courage. But it is not moral courage that is needed. Moral courage stands for principles that have proven their worth in the past. Moral courage stands for righting the wrongs of the world, with both the rights and the wrongs having been defined by time-honored traditions and definitions. Moral courage, in short, champions the tried and the true. But risking a miracle calls for a different kind of courage. It is what Rollo May calls the courage to create. To create new forms, new symbols, new patterns of behavior on which new life can be built.

Neither blueprints nor prescriptions, let alone the requirements of the Law, can call forth this sort of courage. But sometimes stories can. This moving account of a robin found frozen to death illustrates the risk and the courage of passionate living.

With the temperature of 10 below zero, the first Robin was seen in York today. It was found dead on Penn Common.

Call me an old sentimentalist if you will, but this seems to me the most tragic news note of the cold wave. I like people better than robins and there has been widespread and agonizing suffering. But you see, this was the *first* Robin. He was by all odds, the pioneer of his clan. He flew up from the south days, weeks, and months before any reasonable Robin weather was to be expected. Without doubt, the rest tried to discourage him. They spoke of the best recorded experience of birdkind. "Rome wasn't built in a day," some other Robin told him. And no doubt he was advised if he insisted on such precipitous action, he would split the group and no good would come of it. Somehow, I seem to hear him say, "If ten would follow me, I'll call it an army. Are there two who would join me? Or maybe one?"

But the robins all recoiled and clung to their little patches of sun under the southern skies. "Later, maybe," they told him. "Not now." First, there must be a campaign of education.

"Well," replied the Robin who was all for going to York, Pa., without waiting for feathery reinforcements, "I know *one* who will try it. I'm *done* with arguments, so here I go!"

He was so filled with high hopes and dedication that he rose almost with the roar of a partridge. In a few seconds he was a fast moving speck up above the palm trees, and then you couldn't spot him even with field glasses. He was lost in the blue and flying for dear life. "Impetuous, I call it," said one of the elder statesmen while someone took him a worm. "He always did want to show off," announced another. And everyone agreed that no good would come of it.

As it turned out, maybe they were right. It's pretty hard to prove anything has been gained from a robin freezing to death on Penn Common. However, I imagine that he died with a certain sense of elation. None of the rest thought he could get far. The break in the weather turned out to be against him; the break in the weather just turned out to be wrong in that respect. And so, I wouldn't call him a complete failure. When the news gets back home to the robins that didn't go, I rather expect that they will make of him a hero. The elder statesmen will figure that since he's dead his ideas can't longer be dangerous and they cannot deny the lift and the swing of his venture. After all, he was the *first* Robin. He looked for the spring and it failed him . . . . But he is not the victim of caution or dry rot, or doomed to eye strain for too close an attention to leisures. "Here I go," he cries, and I wouldn't be surprised to be told that the first *minute* of flight is reward enough, no matter what follows.

And so, in a metaphorical way of speaking, I bow my head and bow low in the general direction of the ice covered plain which is known as Penn Common. And I think the brief address should carry the statement, "You were the first and after you will come others. They will inherit the grubs and the nests and the comfort, but yours is the glory. *You* are the First Robin.[58]

In this account of a robin found frozen on Penn Common, we find a parable of what passionate living is all about. We also see the great barrier to living passionately is in trying to live safely. When we seek to live securely by doing right or being good or want to be sure of ourselves by never making mistakes, we end up taking few chances. But there is something stultifying about being safe all of the time. And, as Jacques Barzun has observed, there is something characteristic of life that antedates and denies convention. He suggests this is no doubt why saints and apostles more often consort with thieves and prostitutes than with bankers and politicians. There is an undeniable risk to living that, when avoided, exiles us from the exuberance of its adventure.

Another way of living safely is by trying to control life, manipulating it, keeping the lid on, everything done decently and in order, things pigeonholed and categorized. The future, however, is in God's hands—not ours. She keeps disrupting our plans and stirring the nest. She keeps reminding us of the variables. When we try to control life in our wisdom and strength, we gain nothing but anxiety and the anticipation of inevitable trouble. The way to live passionately, therefore, is not to control the river of life nor to push it, but to flow with it. Richard Bach's parable about the river is helpful.

Once there lived a village of creatures along the bottom of a great crystal river.

The current of the river swept silently over them all—young and old, rich and poor, good and evil, the current going its own way, knowing its own crystal self.

Each creature in its own manner clung tightly to the twigs and rocks of the river bottom, for clinging was their way of life, and resisting the current what each had learned from birth.

But one creature said at last, "I am tired of clinging though I cannot see it with my eyes, I trust that the current knows where it is going. I shall let go, and let it take me where it will. Clinging, I shall die of boredom."

The other creatures laughed and said, "Fool! Let go, and that current you worship will throw you tumbled and smashed across the rocks, and you will die quicker than boredom!"

But the one heeded them not, and taking a breath did let go, and at once was tumbled and smashed by the current across the rocks.

Yet in time, as the creature refused to cling again, the current lifted him free from the bottom, and he was bruised and hurt no more.

And the creatures downstream, to whom he was a stranger, cried, "See a miracle! A creature like ourselves, yet he flies! See the Messiah, come to save us all!"

And the one carried in the current said, "I am no more Messiah than you. The river delights to lift us free, if only we dare let go. Our true work is this voyage, this adventure."

But they cried the more, "Saviour!" all the while clinging to the rocks, and when they looked again he was gone, and they were left alone making legends of a Saviour.[59]

It may be that the reason they called Jesus, "Savior," or "Son of God," was not because he had divine blood flowing through his veins, nor because he was born of a virgin. Perhaps it was because he saw more clearly than anyone else the miracle of life, and risked living his fully and passionately. He invites us to do the same, now, while there is yet time.

Notes

1. Henri Troyat, *Tolstoy.* Dell, 1969, p. 349.
2. James W. Fowler, *Stages of Faith: The Psychology of Human Development and the Quest for Meaning.* Harper & Row, 1981, pp. l85f.
3. Gail Sheehy, *Passages.* Bantam Books, 1977, p. 364.
4. From *International Herald Tribune,* Zurich, April 30, 1979.
5. Fowler, *Stages of Faith,* p. 183.
6. Mary Caroline Richards, *Centering on Pottery, Poetry, and the Person.* Wesleyan University Press, Middletown, Connecticut, p. 27.
7. From *Life Maps: Conversations on the Journey of Faith* by Jim Fowler and Sam Keen, Jerome W. Berryman, ed. Copyright © 1978, 1985 Word, Incorporated; used by permission of Word Books, Publisher, Waco, Texas 76796, p. 110.
8. Elizabeth Barrett Browning, "Aurora Leigh." Bk. vii.
9. *Saturday Evening Post,* September, 1980, p. 36.
10. Daniel Iverson, "Spirit of the Living God."
11. Sam Keen, *Beginnings Without End.* Harper & Row, 1975, p. 10.
12. Thomas Kelly, *A Testament of Devotion.* Harper & Row, 1975, p. 56.
13. Keen, *Beginnings Without End,* p. 8.
14. *Ibid.*
15. Carlo Carreto, *Summoned By Love.* Orbis Books, 1978, pp. 44f.
16. Paul Tillich, *The Shaking of the Foundations.* Scribner's, 1948, pp. 111f.

17. Howard Thurman, Disciplines of the Spirit. Friends United Press, 1977, pp. 49f.

18. Sam Keen, *To a Dancing God.* Harper & Row, 1970, p. 1.

19. From *The General Assembly Daily News,* Kansas City, May 24, 1979.

20. Keen, *Beginnings Without End,* p. 61.

21. *Ibid.,* pp. 41f.

22. Karl Barth, *The Word of God and the Word of Man.* Harper & Row, 1957, pp. 38-40.

23. Joseph Campbell, *The Portable Jung.* Viking Press, 1971, pp. 16f.

24. Fowler and Keen, *Life Maps.* p. 149.

25. Alfred Tennyson, "Ulysses." Quoted in *An Anthology of World Poetry,* ed. Mark Van Doren. Harcourt, Brace & Company, 1928, pp. 1207-1209.

26. Fowler and Keen, *Life Maps,* p. 114.

27. Rosemary Daniell, *Fatal Flowers: Sin, Sex and Suicide in the Deep South.* Holt, Rinehart, and Winston, 1980, p. 18.

28. Paul Tillich, "The Nature of a Liberating Conscience," in *Conscience: Theological and Psychological Perspectives,* ed. by Carl Ellis Nelson. Newman Press, 1973, p. 67.

29. Keen, *Beginnings Without End,* pp. 24f.

30. Thurman, *Disciplines of the Spirit,* p. 22.

31. *Time,* May 5, 1980, p. 36.

32. R. Mukerjii, "About School," in *Colloquoy.* Vol. III, No. 1 (January, 1970), p. 2.

33. Keen, *Beginnings Without End,* p. 40.

34. Sheehy, *Passages,* pp. 31, 416.

35. Hannah Tillich, *From Time to Time,* 1973, p. 25. Copyright © by Hannah Tillich. Reprinted with permission of Stein and Day Publishers.

36. Olive Schreiner, *From Man to Man.* Harper & Row, 1927, pp. 458f.

37. Sheehy, *Passages,* p. 362.

38. Source unknown.

39. Hannah Tillich, *From Time to Time,* p. 23.

40. Paul Tillich, *On the Boundary.* Scribners, 1966, p. 13.

41. Thurman, *Disciplines of the Spirit.* p. 47.

42. Anne Morrow Lindbergh, *Gift From the Sea,* Pantheon Books, a division of Random House, Inc., 1978, pp. 86f.

43. Eda LeShan, *The Wonderful Crisis of Middle Age.* Warner Books, 1973, p. 21.

44. William Blake, "Eternity." Quoted in *The Dimensions of Poetry,* ed. James E. Miller, Jr., and Bernice Slote. Dodd, Mead and Company, 1966, p. 338.

45. As quoted from *The Pilgrim Hymnal.* Pilgrim Press, 1958, p. 335.

46. "Gospel of Thomas" 45:30-33, in *The Nag Hammadi Library,* ed. James M. Robinson. Harper & Row, 1977, p. 126.

47. "Dialogue of the Savior" 132:15-16, in *Ibid.,* p. 233.

48. "Dialogue of the Savior" 126:5-8, in *Ibid.,* p. 231.

49. Lowell D. Streiker, *The Promise of Buber.* J. B. Lippincott, 1969, pp. 13-15.

50. Protestant Episcopal Church in the U.S.A., *Book of Common Prayer.* Church Pension Fund, 1945, pp. 23f.

51. Thurman, *Disciplines of the Spirit,* p. 127.

52. Dietrich Bonhoeffer, *Ethics.* The MacMillan Publishing Company, 1964, pp. 151f.

53. Paul Tillich, *The Shaking of the Foundations,* p. 102.

54. May Sarton, *Journal of a Solitude.* W. W. Norton, 1973, pp. 80f.

55. Richard Bach, *Illusions.* Dell, 1979, pp. 161-163.

56. *Time,* August 27, 1973, p. 53.

57. Jurgen Moltmann, *The Passion for Life.* Fortress Press, 1977, p. 37.

58. Newspaper article. Source unknown.

59. Bach, *Illusions,* pp. 14-18.